From a Market Economy to a Finance Economy

FROM A MARKET ECONOMY TO A FINANCE ECONOMY

THE MOST DANGEROUS AMERICAN JOURNEY

A. COSKUN SAMLI

First published in 2013 by
PALGRAVE MACMILLAN®
in the United States—a division of St. Martin's Press LLC,
175 Fifth Avenue, New York, NY 10010.

Where this book is distributed in the UK, Europe and the rest of the world,
this is by Palgrave Macmillan, a division of Macmillan Publishers Limited,
registered in England, company number 785998, of Houndmills,
Basingstoke, Hampshire RG21 6XS.

Palgrave Macmillan is the global academic imprint of the above companies
and has companies and representatives throughout the world.

Palgrave® and Macmillan® are registered trademarks in the United States,
the United Kingdom, Europe and other countries.

ISBN: 978–1–137–32557–0

Library of Congress Cataloging-in-Publication Data

Samli, A. Coskun.
    From a market economy to a finance economy : the most dangerous
American journey / A. Coskun Samli.
        pages cm
    Includes bibliographical references.
        ISBN 978–1–137–32557–0 (alk. paper)
        1. Capitalism—United States. 2. United States—Economic
    conditions—2009– 3. United States—Economic policy—2009–
    4. Finance—United States. 5. Entrepreneurship—United States. I. Title.

HC106.84.S25 2013
330.973—dc23   2012046508

A catalogue record of the book is available from the British Library.

Design by Newgen Imaging Systems (P) Ltd., Chennai, India.

First edition: May 2013

10 9 8 7 6 5 4 3 2 1

This book is dedicated to a most proactive government that worries about the people and the future of the country. Is there such a government out there?

Contents

Exhibits

Preface

During the past two decades or so some scholars maintained that American capitalism will implode because new technologies, often perceived as threats, are blocked; wealth is accumulated in the hands of few who simply are oriented only toward current gains; the education system has stopped producing curious people who want to explore, who are willing to learn more, and who wish to build and make things. The system did not implode but switched from a market economy to a finance economy, which I believe is a preimplosion stage. No country with uneducated people and little curiosity can truly advance. Entrepreneurs who are risk takers, organizers, and doers have been challenged and practically stopped by the most powerful vested interests that have, and are still gaining, even more financial power and are using it to maintain the status quo continually. They are simply motivated by gaining more wealth now.

When I came to the United States some 55 years ago, there was a market economy. Small companies were competing; there was no outsourcing, and only about 15 percent of petroleum was being imported; CEOs did not make much more than their workers; gasoline was about 17 cents a gallon; people bragged about their work and not about the cruises they took; we did not owe money to the Chinese or the Japanese; and there were almost no financial planning and investment companies. That was the time when educational institutions were competing to educate their students better. Doctors used to make home visits with their black bags. The upper limit of income tax was 92 percent. This was a society with unlimited potential and extreme ambition to get better. With the exception of race relations, which have gotten much better with time, the United States was much more of a humane society where people were more valuable than corporate profits. Am I describing a dreamland? No. But I am describing a futuristic, dynamic society with zeal to improve. For instance, in early 1960s I worked with the Office of Consumer Affairs in California. These offices were there in every state. They were closed down by President Reagan, who felt that consumers don't need protection.

Just what happened to the futuristic, dynamic society? It functioned well because the two dominant political parties agreed on the general goals for the society, and even in their approach to fulfill those goals they were not much far apart until about the late 1960s. They were not imagining themselves a football team having a championship match. The progressive American society continued making major progress when president LBJ presented his dream of the great society; unfortunately it was cut short by a "war of choice"—the Vietnam War—and ever since the American society has been moving in the direction of profiteering, greed, and financial control.

Am I being too harsh on the American progress or lack thereof? Perhaps. But how can we improve if we are not critical of our own existing conditions. In 2001 I wrote a book titled *Empowering the American Consumer*, wherein I questioned the purpose of writing it. The answer was that although, on the surface, the American economy seemed to be doing quite well at that time, in reality it had derailed. And if it continued the same way, there was a possibility of disaster. Many powerful firms were focused on their own profits, and were almost forgetting that they owed their very existence to consumers. Instead of generating consumer value they were engaged in what seemed to be an endless merger mania. They were gaining more and more power by buying out their competition and were becoming so powerful that they were terrorizing consumers. Mind you, the conditions then were not nearly as bad as what we are having now in terms of having a finance economy.

To my amazement the current finance economy is antiworker, anticonsumer, anti-immigrants, antipoor, and, above all, antigovernment. Why? The financial giants do not really want to have a higher authority limiting their activities. But I am equally surprised and definitely displeased about how accurate I was in my observations and predictions.

I must reiterate that present-day America is not like what I dreamed when I was very young in a third world country. I used to think that it would be wonderful if there were no greedy elite and people lived in conditions where everyone had equal opportunities to education, to work, to medical care, to advancement, and to share in scientific advancements. The United States appeared to be just such a society where these and other such rights were unquestioned.

In my earlier book I merely question these and other equality conditions. In this book I know they are not there at all.

Just what is needed to be done? From my personal perspective, nothing is likely to be accomplished as long as billionaires and millionaires resist any change in the financing system in the economic activities of the current finance economy. This has to stop. Running our country is not, and should not be, limited to simply creating few high-paying jobs responding to financial pressures. Running our country must involve protecting equal opportunities. Not financial rewards but human values must be the ongoing guideline for future progress shared by all. Equal opportunity in education, in job creation, in industrial advancement should not be controlled by financiers.

When I first came to the United States, I was totally obsessed with the fantastic American education system, which emphasized individual advancement. It taught us that we are not learning simply to get jobs, but to be better citizens and certainly better human beings.

But I keep going back and asking one major question: how did the "one percenters" gain all the power to run our country? Just where is the equal opportunity for the "ninety-nine percenters"? The financiers insist on privatization of practically everything and the "ninety-nine percenters" of our society are proposing social nationalization of certain social activities.

Nationalization: Is It a Pragmatic Solution?

When a function, such as defense, health care, education, or energy, is nationalized all citizens and all consumers share the benefits. The British have nationalized certain industries on and off, thus saving time and cost and solving many other problems. If, for instance, we were to nationalize the health care industry, its efficiency would increase such that instead of about 18 percent of the GDP its cost would be around 8 percent as experienced in Germany, the United Kingdom, or even Israel. Furthermore, the industry, just as in these countries cited and in many others, would cover everyone and would not leave some 45 million people without health care. But the 1 percenters insist on privatization, which is strictly a huge money-making proposition for them and critically enhances the income inequality in our society. If we stop dealing with labels and approach problems realistically, we may decide to nationalize some of the nonprivate issues such as health, defense, education, energy, and the like. We forget that ours is a mixed economy—the biggest attraction for me to study the American economy. Unfortunately, this feature of the economic realities is not even discussed seriously anymore. The 1 percenters have limited the national discourse to profitability and financial issues.

What Is the Role of Corporate Entities?

Much research has dwelled on profitability as an early indicator of "too-big-to-fail" (Greeve 2008). But this is a very complex issue; it is not even possible to measure or estimate if "too-big-to-fail" is a legitimate concept to explore. Would it or would it not be correct to consider size as an asset or a liability? The 1 percenters think it relates strictly to the profitability of the company and the society or the government should not interfere. But what if that profitability is exploiting consumers' rights? Corporate entities must make money by generating consumer value, which I learned very early on, rather than by exploiting them. But do things really happen this way? Unfortunately, the financial giants are making money at the expense of the society as a whole.

This book is a manifesto for what was recently noted as the "99 percenters," who are basically losing ground in a stagnant and troubled economy. Many of my early predictions have become reality, and I sincerely hope that my observations in this book may inspire some people to think and act in favor of the society as a whole rather than support a privileged financial giant that continues to dictate the direction of our economy. Is anybody listening? We must get away from "one dollar one vote" to "one person one vote." Let democracy prevail.

Acknowledgments

This is my twenty-fifth book. It is mainly based on some 14 recessions I lived through and studied. I know perhaps more than most people about recessions and related economic conditions. I hope to share those experiences with you. A book cannot be developed without the help of many people. I hasten to say that this book is the result of my daily discussions and my nightmares. I have difficulty believing that a dynamic society such as ours with so much potential will allow itself to reach such a deteriorating position. My almost daily discussions, at least when he is around, was with my colleague Ron Adams, which help me for my ideas. We have had almost endless discussions as to how our economy can be so great and how sad that it is in the hands of 1 percenters and not showing good progress. My friend Dr. James Gray of Florida Atlantic University has been very instrumental in writing this book. We had many discussions that gave me many good ideas.

My immediate colleagues Dr. El-Ansary and Dr. Kavan were always there to respond to my questions or comments. My friend, coauthor, and scholar Dr. Joe Sirgy of Virginia Tech has always been an inspiration. Dr. Ed Mazze of Rhode Island is usually full of ideas and whenever I talk to him he always shares them with me. My editor Charlotte certainly is the most important inspiration that kept me going. She was most enthusiastic and encouraging about this book. I hope the book will live up to her expectations.

Without help of my research assistants I am not sure I could have accomplished much. Now they have moved on to bigger and better things, but I gratefully acknowledge the assistance I received from John Wells, Weston Probst, and Adenike Olunuga, whose on-and-off work made it possible to get my research together and consistently going in the right direction.

Susan Watts always types my almost illegible handwritten notes. She then constructs it into a book. She is a magic worker. Her husband Bill Watts also deserves much credit for reading the whole manuscript and commenting where they may be possible improvements.

Unlike my previous dean who totally discouraged me from writing books, my current dean Ajay Samant has been very encouraging.

My daughter Dr. Ayla Samli is always interactive and always has many good ideas. My brother Osman Samli lives in Istanbul but he is only a telephone call away and as such has been a critical source of ideas and inspiration.

Finally, but above all, my most important interactive partner and also supporter, my wife Bea Goldsmith who not only read many parts of this book and argued with me, but also gave me the best possible meals, which kept me going. Without the support of the people mentioned here and many others who helped me throughout my long professional life I would not have been very productive—I am truly grateful. I must also add that I am solely responsible for the contents of this book.

I certainly hope that it will stimulate your thoughts and activities to help our country move out of its present doldrums.

A. COSKUN SAMLI
Ponte Vedra, Florida

About This Book

Here is a brief synopsis.

In the preface I talk about my concerns and partially my dreams.

In the introduction the emphasis is particularly on what should be and why.

Chapter 1 deals with just what is happening to the American economy—where some of the real problems are and what appears to be the future.

Chapter 2 explores what it was like earlier and how the conditions are changing and where we are headed.

Chapter 3 goes into one of the most important concepts of the book—the greed factor. If the economy allows greed to take over then the whole system becomes dysfunctional for the majority of the society.

Chapter 4 explores if those giants that are considered to be too big to fail could really survive even if they receive support.

Chapter 5 deals with a summary of what happened during the past five decades or so. It really reflects my professional life.

Chapter 6 points out that one of the major ways of getting out of the current economic doldrums is innovation. It must be strongly stimulated.

Chapter 7 discusses recessions. It points out that they could be eliminated but in some ways they feed the greed factor.

Chapter 8 points out that the society must not be split up. If it is supported by business, education, and government the whole society will benefit.

Chapter 9 finds out that Alice has my concerns. They should be taken very seriously for the future of our society.

Chapter 10 deals with a very important concept, the government. It is maintained that government must be a partner rather than being treated as a foe. The chapter explores the areas where government should be playing a very important role.

Chapter 11 explores just how the current questionable directions can be reversed. This would mean a strong movement toward progress.

Finally, the postscript deals with my wishful thinking about the future of our society, which still has a great potential.

Introduction

Robert B. Reich (2010) raises a fundamental question: "[W]hat and whom is an economy for?" The answer will be a most shocking "for only a privileged few." At the writing of this book, the American economy is not doing very well. Not only is it displaying the worst income distribution of all industrialized countries, it is also experiencing a most unusual situation similar to the kind we encounter in children's stories dealing with evil kings and ruthless emperors who take all of the riches and enslave their people with the aim of getting richer. Unfortunately, what is experienced in the American economy is not a theme in a storybook; it is real. The mighty American economy had reached a meltdown point in 2008; it has not been recovering strongly. The Federal government bailed out the financial sector, in the auto industry, interest rates are nearing zero, and more and more Americans are reaching the level of poverty. Incomes for those who are lucky enough to have a job are going down, major jobs in the economy are being exported to lower-income countries, and national indebtedness is reaching an uncontrollable level.

The political arm of the society is totally dysfunctional and there does not seem to be any relief in sight. Just what happened to the society that used to be the envy of the world for many decades? The American economy is taking a very dangerous path. Modern world history is full of examples of how such situations eventually become class warfare and moreover how nations get broken and disappear. In the name of freedom, too much propaganda is trying to prevent any remedial activity in favor of 1 percenters receiving more and more without any consideration for the future of the country and well-being of the 99 percenters. However, again at the writing of this book, about 1 percent of the American population, called "1 percenters" throughout this book, is receiving roughly 92 percent of the total American GDP while the rest of the society, named "99 percenters" throughout, is receiving about 8 percent of the total GDP. This situation is not fair; it is totally biased as if the whole society is enslaved and working for the evil emperor mentioned earlier. But, above all, this is not a sustainable situation. Something very dangerous is likely to take place. But instead of analyzing the root causes of this intolerable situation and determining what needs to be done to reverse the situation before it is too late, the prevailing conditions are supporting the same destructive pattern that may eventually ruin our society.

This book is about exploring the root causes of the current situation and attempts to identify ways in which we can reverse it. Not only is some discipline in economic, political, and social activities needed, but we also need to go back to our glorious years of innovation. During the past half century the American economy moved forward with its innovative capabilities. At this point though, the 1 percenters are not even thinking of innovation as one of the cures for the very questionable current situation. American innovativeness is dwindling without any financial and economic support. Innovation is not the complete answer, but it can make a major contribution toward normalizing our society. This is because an innovative breakthrough can bring tremendous economic benefits to our struggling society—an idea explored very carefully in this book.

Steve Jobs, one of the most well-known innovators of our times, repeatedly emphasized the need for a product-oriented culture (Nussbaum 2005). This activity is outsourced by the 1 percenters. In a more elaborate manner Kao (2007) stated that innovative countries constantly lay emphasis on creating the desired future. In this sense innovation is a state of evolution that cannot be ignored or allowed to be side-tracked. But while the good jobs are being exported, educational budgets are reduced, and government funds are redirected to the military, American innovativeness is bound to be totally deteriorating. At a time of great recession, there is no room for innovational efforts. The recession is explored in detail in this book and the conclusion is that recessions are man-made and they benefit the 1 percenters.

As Manu (2007) stated, without innovative breakthroughs, which are mostly displayed by new and radical product development, it will be impossible to solve the most pressing economic problems that are threatening the future of our society.

In this book it is posited that the dwindling motivation for innovation and deteriorating economic conditions are due to a major negative force: the American market economy is becoming a finance economy and the 1 percenters have no interest in stopping this trend. The finance-driven economy is not paying attention to the general well-being of the 99 percenters and the future of the American economy. This pattern must be reversed as quickly as possible; in a very modest way this book aims at doing just that.

However, there is almost no indication that the aforementioned trend is now being reversed. It must be understood that if the consumers at the basic level of our economy are gainfully employed, are consuming at normal levels, are enjoying some income increases, and are experiencing job security, not only would the quality of life in our society be enhanced, but it would be very beneficial to the financial giants as well. However, if the society moves primarily in the direction of and to benefit the financial giants rather than to create a progressive and prosperous economy, it leads to a very dangerous dichotomy between haves and have-nots. Thus, what it needs is a bottom-up orientation to benefit the society to begin with rather than benefiting the financial giants, which is top-down. Bottom-up orientation is what we need to go back to rather than the top-down orientation, which is predominant in our society and is causing a lot of damage (Samli 2001).

Building Wealth in a Society

If businesses want to grow rapidly with high profit margins, they must take advantage of disruptive technologies and emphasize radical innovations. All other activities are slow-growth and low-rate-of return types. But those gains must start from the bottom where people are employed and share the benefits of growth (Thurow 2000; Samli 2009a).

In fact, there is a basic orientation as to how to generate wealth and properly distribute it. Exhibit I.1 illustrates just how the whole process begins. Without creating and maintaining public order the society is helpless, it cannot make any progress. Political and/or social unrest can definitely interfere with the economic progress of the society. In fact, even an advanced society such as Japan stopped its marvelous economic progress during the late twentieth century as its political picture became unstable.

In order to maintain public order, as can be seen in exhibit I.1, it is necessary to have a power structure within and outside the country. A police force maintains internal order, and an army provides protection against external aggression. Naturally, both power structures are based on the guidelines identified by a legal structure that will protect the population and encourage economic progress. The legal and power structures must provide the necessary orientation for progress. Kotler, Jatusripitak, and Maesiencel (1997) discuss the structures and the orientation that exist in the four Asian tigers (Singapore, Taiwan, Hong Kong, and South Korea), which may be considered a very valuable and viable model. In all these countries there is an active and fully functioning elite, which provides the necessary impetus for economic progress that can be described in terms of creating wealth and distributing it equitably. If the conditions of public order are met, then it is critical to redirect much of the attention to the infrastructure. In other words, reasonably powerful local governments and economic power are the ingredients necessary to create wealth in a society.

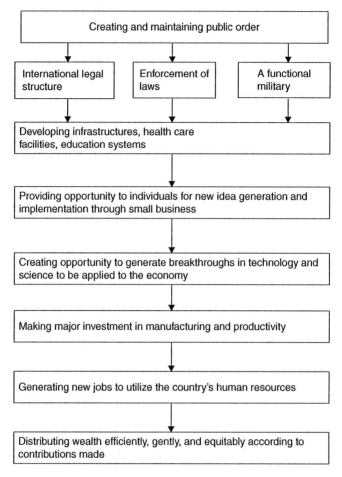

Exhibit I.1 Generating wealth.
Source: Adapted and revised from Samli (2009a).

Developing the Infrastructure

Economic progress in terms of wealth creation and its distribution cannot happen without a functional and advanced infrastructure. Unfortunately, this all-important concept, most of the time, is put on the back burner by the prevailing financial powers. But then, in their rather simplistic model, the 1 percenters do not allow the government to make progress in infrastructure development (Stiglitz 2002). But in reality governments are, and must be, key players in the development and maintenance of infrastructures since they are costly and do not generate revenues particularly in the short run.

Without an infrastructure that generates energy, facilitates mobility, creates information, and supports basic facilities that are needed for manufacturing the society cannot make economic progress. The infrastructure that is so necessary but so unprofitable to develop efficiently by the private sector, particularly by financial giants, almost by definition, becomes the government's purview.

Of course, in order to develop an effective labor force as well as a healthy and informed population, it is essential that health care facilities and educational systems are properly functional and accessible. A well-functioning infrastructure is more than essential in wealth creation and distribution.

Generating Breakthroughs

Earthshaking new ideas such as developing a sequel to Einstein's $E = MC^2$ may not be possible or even necessary. But generating information technology wireless communication means or new wonder drugs to cure major diseases, in short radical technology, is a must. Even milder innovations in improving food value while reducing their costs, creating and using more renewable energy, and the like are extremely critical to generating wealth. It is important that the society encourages entrepreneurs to generate and distribute new products that would enhance the quality of life for all. But if an innovation culture is discouraged and blocked, then the society suffers. There are possibilities to develop radical innovations that would yield economic wealth for the society in the long run but they are mostly blocked by financiers who would like to see immediate financial benefits.

Investment in Manufacturing

It is not outsourcing but producing necessities as well as luxuries within the country that is a must to create wealth for the whole society. As wealth accumulates, it is important that a major proportion of it be funneled into investment in manufacturing and also in housing. But the rich in our society, despite the propaganda in favor of the opposite, do not invest in manufacturing. If there is more and more wealth accumulating in the hands of the 1 percenters who are financial giants, there will not be enough to invest and modernize manufacturing. This can be a very critical disruption in a society's economic progress. But again the very rich are very comfortable in their current situation; they would not be very motivated to invest in manufacturing as they are making more money without it. They certainly prefer to play the stock market and participate in other financial activities. The people who are likely to invest in production and take chances are the middle-income entrepreneurial group that has the ambition to get ahead. But ambition alone is not enough; the conditions for an innovation culture must be present and be supportive of this group. Such ambitious entrepreneurial groups are essential for generating the desired economic advancement.

Unfortunately, our manufacturing has been outsourced to such an extent that it is not clear if we can produce the basic essentials for our society reasonably and efficiently.

Utilizing the Country's Human Resources

At the writing of this book, an estimated 8.2 percent are unemployed, a few million are underemployed, meaning they are not working full time, and a few million have given up looking for a job. Such unused or wasted human resources make a society progressively poor. But if the financial sector that has become so powerful and is in charge of the overall economic activity is doing quite well, as it is in the short run, the human resources are likely to remain underutilized and the economic progress for the society as a whole takes on a disruptive pattern.

Only if we rely more on the ambition factor of the people and generate jobs for all competent and fully trained workers can we get moving again. This means we must get away from a zero-sum society orientation where the focus is on receiving a greater share of the economic activity at the cost of many rather than on thinking how to make the economy as a whole grow. One group must not think that it can advance only if the other groups lose, which means a zero-sum orientation.

Distributing Wealth Efficiently, Gently, and Equitably

The last step in exhibit I.1 is just that. If the generated wealth in a society accumulates only in the hands of a few the whole process described in the exhibit comes to a halt. Leveling the playing field, giving the poor a greater stake, promoting a more liberal democracy, and encouraging the dominant rich elite to be more participatory partners are essential (Chua 2003).

Leveling the playing field is making sure that everyone has access to better education and better access to employment. Educating the population as opportunities are created is simply the most important activity that would narrow the gap between the haves and have-nots.

Giving the poor a greater stake in the total economy and bringing them into the mainstream of economic activity would benefit the whole society. There may be different ways to achieve this goal but what is important here is making sure that all people, not only the financially privileged, count.

Promoting a liberal democracy implies that not only the privileged financial giants, but the whole society counts. A dynamic society such as ours needs dynamic leadership but the financial giants prefer the "status quo." They block a dynamic liberal government.

The dominant, rich elite, unfortunately, are much more involved in getting a larger chunk of the GDP instead of worrying about the future growth and prosperity of the society. There are ample examples to show that when the talented and powerful financial elite puts its efforts into economic growth for the country rather than receiving more money in the short run, it proves to be extremely beneficial to the society (Chua 2003; Samli 2009a). But this is not happening in our country.

Generating and distributing wealth efficiently and equitably, without a doubt, is the most important solution to economic inequalities and cultural clashes.

The model presented in exhibit I.1 is a very workable one; up until about four decades ago, in the prevailing market economy, it worked reasonably well. But the current finance economy of the recent decades does not go any further than the first step in exhibit I.1. Thus, the continuity implied in the exhibit is simply not present. That is the great danger that instigated this book.

Summary

The American economy is on an extremely dangerous path. It has moved from a market orientation to a finance orientation. In this introduction it is maintained that this movement must be reversed before it is too late. It points out that the financial giants who are referred to as "1 percenters" are in charge. They pay more attention to receiving more money in the short run rather than being concerned about the society and its progress in the long run. The model presented in this chapter worked for very many years. But instead of developing it further, at this point in time it is totally dormant.

Chapter 1

American Market Economy: Quo Vadis

General Electric, the company that made light bulbs since their innovation, in 2007 decided to begin outsourcing its next generation of bulbs to China, which caused many job losses in the United States.

The recovery from the 2008–2009 recession has been sketchy at best. But the business sector has been in the black. The stock market recovered, corporate profits went up, but the job market and domestic investment activity did not recover. They remained drastically low.

The American Medical Association (AMA) prevents extra competition by using its political influence to prevent nurses, physician's assistants, and qualified others from providing services such as midwifery or massage therapy to keep prices high by reducing the choice.

Our finance system has become essentially a secret casino, which belongs to the mafia. The world's wealthiest companies and individuals in that casino bet with trillions of dollars of other people's money. If they lose they expect to be bailed out by the government, but if they are making much money they are totally antigovernment.

Millions of homes were sold at exorbitant prices to people who cannot afford them. The end result is that millions of homes are locked into contracts to pay hugely inflated housing prices. But the market value of these houses are much lower.

These are only a few examples of how the American economy is becoming anticonsumer, antiworker, and antihuman values. It has become mean and calloused (Ratigan 2012).

If our economy can be coined as a market economy, then we have to understand what it really means and how that meaning can be implemented to the reality of our country's daily life. The market economy is based on human values, makes people work, and working people get fair reward for their efforts.

The market economy is the epitome of functionality of an economy. In the final analysis any economy must be functioning at the point that a market system requires. Here, perhaps most of the people in this country have the following question in their minds: Just what is a market economy and how does it function?

The Market Economy

Unlike the prehistoric alternative of being gatherers and the more recent one of being agrarian economies the market economy strictly deals with people. It makes people satisfy their needs by having access to products and services. The market economy makes these goods and services readily available at prices the consumers can afford. In the market economy satisfying consumer needs through effective marketing creates a reward that is called profit. Naturally, the market economy must emphatically emphasize that marketing efforts be fair and reasonably profitable rather than exploitative. In other words, the market economy must be beneficial to all people of the society rather than to only totally profit-oriented people or financiers.

A Fully Functioning Market System

If the market economy is as functional as it may be presented in economics books it will accomplish numerous basic tasks.

The market economy is basically an arrangement that allows buyers and sellers to exchange products and services for money (O'Sullivan and Sheffrin 2001). If this basic condition prevails then a number of additional conditions emerge. Wilfredo Pareto summarized these conditions under the title of "Paretian optimality." These are: making available the greatest volume of goods for most people in the society, which means, in Pareto's terminology, no one could be made better off without making someone else worse off. This further means allocations of economic resources in such a way that some people cannot be better off without making others worse off (Pieters 2005–2012). Thus, a perfectly competitive market system is an ideal system where no player could be better off without another becoming worse off. If this is the ideal goal for a market economy how do we explain the aforementioned practices? The market economy should function to reach or at least come closer to that goal and improve the quality of life for all.

Perhaps Pareto's optimality cannot be achieved totally, but the market economy, at least, could function in that direction, even though ultimate equilibrium as Pareto envisioned cannot be readily achieved.

As opposed to such theoretical equilibrium goals, the market economy followed a series of certain functions through organized behavior systems, which are firms or enterprises (Alderson 1965). What these firms were involved in has been called marketing, but despite the complexity of the market economy, a marketing theory did not attract much attention. It was the earlier work of Alderson (1957) that established the ground work for a theory of marketing that presented a theoretical orientation for the firm's functionality. From that perspective the firms in the market economy started producing for certain specific groups of consumers; they made the products and services available by storing, transporting, and delivering of goods. But as these activities continued the market economy started showing favoritism and making some firms big, successful, and rich as many others failed. This pattern disrupted the possibility of achieving Pareto's optimality and diverted the market economy in time to become a finance economy with many key problems for the majority of people in a society, which are discussed in the following paragraphs.

As the market economy became more complicated about less than one hundred years ago marketing emerged as a discipline. Marketing discipline continued from where microeconomics left off. This primarily meant the market system moved in the direction of being efficient, which meant being able to produce greater output with reduced input. Efficiency from a micromarketing perspective, unfortunately, lost the possibility of approaching Pareto optimality, in favor of making more money for individual firms. Many industrial giants functioned in the market system in the way that marketing discipline coined it as being involved in practicing extreme marketing for profit only, rather than for the enhancement of quality of life.

The marketing discipline, although exploring possibilities to constantly perform well in the market economy, did not make a critical difference between the short run and the long run. Thus, the practice of business did not follow the direction of Pareto's optimality. Profiteering and discrimination against consumers brought the market economy to a point where strong deviations from the earlier market economy advocated by Adam Smith (1779) took place. These deviations were termed "pathological" (Samli and Sirgy 1982). Five pathological conditions were identified:

1. Inadequate levels of raw materials, energy, and other resources.
2. Inappropriate forms of these items.
3. Inadequate levels of marketing information.
4. Wrong direction of prevailing marketing philosophy.
5. Abnormal international marketing practices.

These pathological conditions individually as well as together created a movement at odds with an optimally functioning system.

The situations reached a point where President John F. Kennedy (1963) had to establish the conditions necessary to eliminate discrimination and enhance consumer protection. These were:

1. The right to be informed.
2. The right to choose.
3. The right to be protected.
4. The right to be heard.

None of these conditions have been eliminated (Samli 1992); thus, the market system slowly but surely has been getting away from benefitting the consumer. Even though the marketing discipline had been roughly followed, certain parts of the market economy, inspired perhaps by Pareto's optimality, appeared to be disappearing. Quite ignored is the fact that the market system worked on the emphasis of efficiency. But the concept of efficiency has been misconstrued. It was interpreted as trying to make more and more money without considering the society's well-being. The conditions or activities that worked for the enhancement of the society and for improving economic conditions for all have been ignored. As microeconomics gave way to micromarketing, macroeconomics and macromarketing conditions to achieve Pareto's optimality appeared to be forgotten or totally deemphasized.

This situation has led to deemphasizing the qualities of a market economy of promoting economic advancement and enhancement of quality of life in the long run. Instead, the total activity was focused on making as much money as possible and not considering consumer well-being or the advancement of the society. While productivity in the industries increased continually, this was translated into more and more profit for some enterprises rather than increased employment that would benefit the whole society (Bloomberg Business Week 2012a).

This short-run emphasis and the economic regression of our society can be attributed to the dramatic change of our economy from a market to a finance economy. This change is primarily based on two key factors: First, the micromarketing discipline during the immediate past half century has developed a number of techniques that have enhanced the financial sector's ability to make a lot of money; second, an unprecedented greed factor appeared to control the market system.

From a Market Economy to a Finance Economy

During the past three decades or so the American economy has been increasingly guided by the financial sector. This is partially due to the fact that the marketing discipline has developed a high level of sophistication that has been very supportive of the financial sector to make more money in the short run without considering the consumer quality of life and economic progress. Sophisticated techniques of determining market segments, catering to their particular needs, and advanced communication techniques have been generating outstanding profits, which are not benefiting the average consumer or the society in general. Excessive profitability appeared in the national economy in terms of inequalities in income distribution. This inequality in income distribution has become more and more imbalanced over the years. The gross domestic product (GDP) of the American society is primarily concentrated in the hands of about 1 percent of the population. Currently, it has been stated that about 350 people or families in the United States have more money and wealth than 150 million Americans; similarly, the top 1 percent owns more wealth and receives more income than the remaining 99 percent of the society. This basically means that the market economy is in the hands of a group of finance people and is neither reaching the average consumer nor benefiting the whole population. It may be reiterated that the market economy is becoming a finance economy; it is getting further and further away from Pareto's optimality, which in fact is the picture of the ideal market economy's performance. As the finance economy conditions described earlier prevailed, it became even worse in terms of creating more difficult conditions for the average consumer. Consumers found it more difficult to find better jobs. Their job security almost totally disappeared. Their average incomes stagnated. These conditions indicated that the American society was facing an intolerable economic predicament. The American economy should be brought back to a balanced situation so that it levels the playing field and all people have equal opportunity to economic well-being. In short a well-functioning market economy, which caters to consumer well-being and to the economic progress of the society rather than making only a select few extremely wealthy, is needed.

The Dangers of Proceeding as a Finance Economy

At least three very critical areas must be considered as the finance economy endangers our economic well-being and therefore our future. First, money accumulates in the hands of a very small group. Second, unchecked financial economy encourages and supports what this author has termed the "greed factor," which simply indicates making money almost endlessly and harming the rest of the society is perfectly alright without any checks, regulations, and financial conditions. Third, and perhaps the most critical, in the long run the financial economy allows key corporations to grow without almost any social responsibility to the point where they become too big to fail. The author maintains that this finance economy concept must be reversed and the too-big-to-fail concept must be described also as *too big to succeed.*

Money Accumulating in the Hands of a Few

Those who understand recessions know that generating effective demand is the key weapon against recession. In fact, it has been stated that unemployment is a failure of demand (Reich 2010). This means consumers must have money and some degree of job security. Only under these conditions can new jobs be created. Generating effective demand when the money is accumulating in the hands of very few millionaires and billionaires, almost by definition, indicates that there is no opportunity for creating new jobs. Consumers simply do not have enough money to buy things and demand more and better products and services. Thus, it is extremely difficult to create more new jobs, which is the most important or even perhaps the only way to keep recessions at bay. An important secondary impact of money accumulating in the hands of a group of extremely rich people is that they do not have a high propensity to consume (Dillard 1948; Keynes 1936). This means the rich do not have to spend money immediately and when they do spend, it may go to stock markets, or other nonessentials, and therefore, not at all be utilized in a most effective way. The poorer consumers will spend money wisely on major essentials and simulate basic demand, which is needed to create jobs. This whole process will take place in the shortest run.

But, it must be reiterated that the finance economy is not oriented to generate more employment, economic progress, and enhancement of consumer quality of life. This is due to the fact that, at least partially, marketing is not marketed properly and the economy is going in a rather questionable direction. The financial giants are chasing money as much as possible rather than improving the quality of life for all. There is a key issue that needs to be resolved. As has been established earlier, should the market economy become more and more a finance economy or should there be certain conditions initiated so that the American economy will become once again a market economy, working toward Pareto's optimality? If the resurrection of the market economy is desired then a more difficult question will be raised in terms of just how to accomplish such a difficult goal. These issues are considered further, but two more critical danger areas connected to the finance economy must be considered. The first of these two is the greed factor.

The Emergence of Greed Factor

Perhaps one of the most critical developments, which happens to be the most dangerous, is that the finance economy fully supports what is termed here as the "greed factor." As the economy becomes more and more finance controlled the greed factor is considered as a positive feature for individual decision-makers who are the movers and shakers of the American society. Rand (1957) advocated that greed is a very important characteristic of successful individuals. However, it is important to explore other alternatives. Samli (2009) maintained that capitalism provides two opposing alternatives. The first is that capitalism cultivates ambition. In fact, it is reasonable to maintain that the American economy, in the hands of ambitious entrepreneurs, made tremendous progress during the era informally ending by the late 1970s or so. Ambitious entrepreneurs started new businesses and created jobs for millions. This orientation cultivated and strengthened the market economy. But capitalism, if there are no checks and balances, no regulations, and perhaps no certain conditions, can facilitate the growth of the greed factor. As opposed to small entrepreneurial and ambitious start-ups, the greed factor provides opportunity not to pay attention to others and accumulate financial power at the expense of others. The greed factor encourages certain already powerful people to almost stop the ambitious entrepreneurs and make more money by blocking them. They buy out these ambitious entrepreneurs and put them out of existence or use their efforts for their own benefit. As they benefit by receiving wealth and profit, the society loses. At the writing of this book the American economy is experiencing a dichotomy of a very small but extremely rich group named "1 percenters" controlling the society. The remaining 99 percent of the population are members of a disappearing middle class and an emerging very large poor class. The 99 percenters are notably trying to reverse this pattern. This situation will not change or will not be reversed unless there are some regulations controlling financial activity in the society such as a progressive tax system and special support for ambitious entrepreneurs. One of the most critical features of the greed factor is that those strong supporters are constantly doing propaganda about and supporting privatization in the name of freedom. Privatization cannot possibly handle society's major activity needs such as education, defense, infrastructure development, energy, health care, and the like. But privatization can create endless financial benefits for a few.

Too Big to Fail or Too Big to Succeed

Perhaps one of the worst aspects of a finance economy is the encouragement of begetting more power. Some of the corporations in our society have become so large that in the 1990s a term was created to define them: "too big to fail." This concept has been coming up each time there is a recession. It must be reiterated that although some politicians call them job creators, large corporations, particularly in recessions, do not create jobs. There is always news of Sears and HP laying off thousands of people and the list simply goes on. Friedman (2010) pointed out that between 1985 and 2005 about 45 million jobs were created in the United States. Almost all of them were created by companies that are small, entrepreneurial, and young. Once again while gigantic American companies cut out jobs to make themselves survivable and richer, the small entrepreneurial ones created jobs. But the financial economy totally approves of these entrepreneurial companies being purchased by the giants and laying off of people to maintain profit. The American economy since about the early 1980s has been approving the financial piracy that is merger mania. The young, innovative entrepreneurial companies, which would be totally supported in a market economy, are being bought out and put out to pasture in the finance economy. Thus, at the point of writing this book, small entrepreneurial companies are either considered to be a danger or a small gold mine and hence are purchased by the too-big-to-failers. It must be further recognized that this endless merger mania is basically disrupting the American innovativeness. The old adage of if you cannot beat them you join them has been replaced in the finance economy as just buy them out and perhaps put them out of their misery. At a time when the BRIC (Brazil, Russian, India, and China) countries are making major progress, the finance economy is blocking the potential of American progress. During the era of market economy American society enjoyed innovations and creativity, which is strongly related to economic prosperity. But under the finance economy there has been almost a war declared on the middle class and labor. The middle class, which is the stabilizing and the growth factor in the American economy, at the point of this writing, is about to become totally extinct; its members will go below the poverty lines. That is a dangerous trend for our economy. In fact, Reich (2007) stated that capitalism has become more responsive to financial powers than democracy, meaning that money has become more important than freedom. The bailout program by President Obama has worked some, which has stimulated the thinking that with the government's partnership the finance economy can work (Engardio 2008). However, such wishful thinking would not take away the tremendous dangers that the finance economy posits. This is a major disruption of the expected American economic progress.

Perhaps one of the major issues, which is not carefully researched in the finance economy, is the dichotomy of too-big-to-fail versus too-big-to-succeed. Are the companies too big to fail but also can they succeed with this size?

More on Too-Big-to-Fail or Too-Big-to-Succeed

The gigantic corporations, which have been pushing for more and more financial gains, have been creating many very serious problems. The author maintains that perhaps the most critical problem of the gigantic corporations is their size. It is considered here that these corporate entities all have optimal sizes, which are not carefully explored and identified. But beyond that optimal size they may not be functional enough to contribute to the economic progress of the country.

As early as late 1970s George Romney maintained that GM is extremely big and must be broken into a number of companies to become much more functional and productive. However, as the economy moved in the direction of being finance oriented such considerations totally disappeared. The gigantic corporations, even though not readily discussed in the literature or almost totally under-researched, are suffering from multiple problems. We consider these problems in two basic categories—external and internal. These are discussed in chapter 4 in detail. Only a brief orientation is presented here.

External Problems

The size creates numerous external problems regarding the company's markets. The industrial giants are too far from their markets, and they do not readily comprehend some of the quick and unexpected changes that are happening in their markets. They have difficulty making quick decisions to counteract the critical and perhaps unexpected market conditions. They have little understanding of remote and diversified third-world markets. They typically lack sensitivity regarding what third-world markets need. Finally, they are not innovative in dealing with varying demands in scattered, small, and unique third-world countries (Samli 2009b). The lack of ability to cope with very small, dynamic, and diverse global markets makes the global or national giants quite incompetent, resulting in ineffectiveness in contributing to the well-being of consumers and economic growth.

Internal Problems

Internally, the global and national giants have many problem areas, several of which are not identified or carefully explored. Since this topic is discussed in detail in chapter 4 of this book, only a few of these problems are identified in this introductory chapter.

In addition to being very big and hence having many layers of organizational activity that block fast decision-making and create less-than-adequate decision-making speed, there are internal politics. It is, for instance, quite possible that a number of internal candidates are competing for a higher management position and therefore are promoting their favorite projects and trying to block their competitors' projects. Similarly, internally, people at higher levels trying to excel within the organization may promote their own projects that happen to be less effective than those the competitors may have. This situation may cause some degree of internal confusion and may block the best opportunities for the company to make the needed progress.

Sull (2005) puts forth many other internal antiprogress possibilities such as being too tied to the existing technology and not allowing technological progress to enter the organizational arena.

Finally, picking the right person for the job could create much internal political conflict.

As we discuss the problems with the finance economy and reevaluate the conditions, we can easily see that the finance economy has many aspects that are likely to make the American economy a member of the second-class economy countries. Thus, it is extremely critical to revive and revitalize the market economy alternative. This will take some very major changes in the American politics and the American economy.

The Market Economy Alternative

Just what would happen if the American economy, once again, were to become a market economy? With some degree of wishful thinking the author believes the following are likely to take place.

First, there will be more entrepreneurial support. Entrepreneurial entities will not be allowed to be bought out. Furthermore, there will be more encouragement for radical innovations that would empower the economy and create a powerful stance for the American economy in the global arena.

Second, with better distribution of incomes, there would be more buying power for the middle-income group, which will create many new jobs. Income distribution will become more normal for a progressive society such as ours and this would psychologically encourage workers to work harder and receive more value for their efforts.

Third, the power of the greed factor will be somewhat reduced by a more progressive income tax and more carefully constructed regulations to encourage not the greedy but the ambitious.

Fourth, the corporate entities will be encouraged not to get unmanageably large. Instead they will be encouraged to be lean, mean competing machines. As a result there will be more competition, which will aid the country's economic growth and help to normalize the income distribution.

Fifth, perhaps above all, more marketing will be practiced and researched to enhance the prevailing quality of life, rather than helping to perform more financial manipulations and to create more wealth for a small group of people while the rest of the society is being ignored.

Just how could the American economy go back to being a market economy rather than a finance economy?

The first thing, as Engardio (2008) suggested, is the recognition and cooperation of public and private sectors rather than trying to do away with the public sector. In such a case the government would play a role of leadership and protecting all consumers rather than simply supporting the finance group's position.

As has been hinted throughout this chapter if the prevailing lawlessness and capitalizing on laws of the jungle are to be replaced by reasonable laws and regulations dealing with the well-being of the consumers and the society, the American society will reach, although belatedly, the twenty-first century. The regulations against financial evil, which creates more and more wealth for the 1 percent group against 99 percent of the population's well-being, will help to go back to being a market economy. Again, as hinted in the chapter, entrepreneurial efforts will have to be treated carefully and forcefully since that group will be the rescuer of the society and create wealth as well as jobs. Similarly, the features of the market economy must be more readily emphasized by the academic world. Not only the money-making aspects of marketing but also more emphasis on innovation, efficiency, enhancement of quality of life, and economic progress will have to be laid and carefully instructed.

Summary

This chapter is perhaps the most important synopsis of what has been the recent pattern and what is happening to the American society. Two most important points are posited. First, the American economy must not be controlled or directed by the finance people. Maintaining that if you take the government out of the economy, the remaining would resolve all the problems is a very old and a totally unsubstantiated point of view. It must be dramatically stated that the American society and indeed the world would not have a future with the presence of a general orientation preferring the future and not caring about the financial orientation.

Finally, this chapter indirectly implies that the greed factor through the financial push will not take place. This means that the corporate entities must manage not by the bottom line dictated by the financial powers but must manage for a bottom line. The bottom line here is fairness to all consumers and equal opportunity for the consumers. These will regenerate the market economy for the economy and for the future of this country.

The discussion presented in this chapter is expanded and critically developed throughout this book.

Chapter 2

The Disappearing Magic of the Market Economy

Starting with World War II pressures, the American economy bloomed until about 1982. During that period competition and ambition supported by an understanding and not totally indoctrinated federal government performed near miracles.

The United States became number one in the world in industrial development, producing the most college graduates, being the most innovative nation, a country experiencing the fastest economic growth, having the best medical system, and the like. At the time, to an outsider such as the present author, this was the movement to perfection. In addition to the prevailing ambition the political system was not totally divided. In fact, although there were differences in implementation plans the two political parties were not too far from each other and did not block each other's activities. The market economy that was managed from the bottom-up by having support for start-ups created more innovation and entrepreneurship and functioned quite well.

During this era, competition at all levels of the economy trimmed the budgets and improved economic opportunities. Small start-up entrepreneurs received help and the total earnings of a CEO were not tremendously different from the total earnings of labor. There appeared to be a positive functionality in the market economy driven by ambition, hard work with a politically smooth and supportive atmosphere. This total picture may have been called the magic of a well-functioning market economy. However, by the beginning of 1980s this whole picture started reversing itself. Too much political propaganda and increases in the greed factor created most favorable conditions for a few in the society. The American economy started creating fortunes as the society may not make progress as a whole, and other related conditions discussed in this chapter started converting the market economy to a finance economy.

Underlying Forces

Some years ago in one of my books (Samli 1991) I wrote a section titled "Mary, Mary Quite Contrary How Does Your Economy Grow?" It may be shocking to realize that the forces that have been ailing the American economy were already in action then. My statement continued as follows: "Mary your economy grows not by derailing the current American economy, not by discriminating against the consumers, not by allowing anarchy to take over the economy and not at all by being inactive in sociopolitical and economic arenas." I should have included forcefully that your economy cannot grow by undermining or by derailing the American workers. I continued, however, by saying that: "Mary, your economy will grow if consumers, and workers, added in this analysis, are empowered. If people are given equal opportunity to choose, to advance, to work and to accomplish your economy will grow." It further continued: "Mary your economy will grow if competition is not undermined, if economic power is not allowed to concentrate in the hands of a few, e.g. one percenters, indiscriminately." These were the major forces to be reinforced and not to be abandoned. In short, the advice to Mary summarized the conditions that made the market economy grow from the bottom-up until around the early 1980s.

Just What Went Wrong

Perhaps the most debated and the most occupying issue during the total history of the American economy is the definition of "free enterprise system." Two completely opposing orientations have sponsored big debates and related political and economic action. The first orientation may be summarized by Gaski (1985) where he stated that the economy is in a natural equilibrium and as such it is sacrosanct. If left alone it will perform perfectly well. It is a product of almost a divine dispensation. The opposing point of view is articulated by Dugger (1989), who points out that such beliefs lead to "enabling myths": "sacrosanctity" and "perfectness" of the economy are myths. But these myths are enabling the upper strata in our society to maintain dominance over the lower strata. He further maintained that those who benefit from the institutionalized status quo, the critical 1 percenter position at the writing of this book, believe that they benefit because their personal gifts or efforts merit it. But this basic orientation ignores two major facts: (1) people are educable, and hence those skills acclaimed to be personal gifts are not totally unique and many others can possess them through training; and (2) many people do not have equal opportunity to obtain them (Samli 2001). Meaning basically that the play field is not leveled and hence many deserving people are not able to develop the skills to perform at higher levels in our economy. During the past three decades or so Gaski's position has become consistently stronger, which actually indicated the American economy's transition from a market economy to a finance economy.

The Three Major Trends

The financialization of the economy was accelerated by at least three major trends: (1) deregulation, (2) tax cuts, and (3) merger mania. All three of these trends created major changes in the management

Deregulation
- Freedom to perform questionable practices
- Lack of regulations in critical areas
- Simulating the greed factor
- Lack of control

Tax cuts
- Creating greater economic inequality
- Encouraging outsourcing
- Emergence of equity finance companies

Merger mania
- Purchasing lean, mean, competing machines
- Disrupting the major innovational activities
- Reducing industrial competitiveness

Exhibit 2.1   The three trends and their questionable impact.

of our economy and contributed to the disappearance of the magic of market economy.

Exhibit 2.1 summarizes the key impacts of each of the three trends.

Deregulation

Perhaps quite innocently and with good intentions President Carter started planting the seeds of deregulation. Indeed perhaps there were some regulations without which individual businesses could function better. However, this situation did not apply to all regulations. Starting the elimination of regulations almost across the board did not necessarily increase competition nor did it create a better functioning market economy.

As indicated in the exhibit, deregulation opened up the possibilities of some people performing certain questionable activities. Among many such activities, mergers and acquisitions with and of competition resulted in companies gaining extraordinary financial powers and starting to convert ambition to greed. Lack of regulations or lack of enforcement of existing regulations started creating environmentally unfriendly practices, which were financially extremely desirable. Instead of enhancing and strengthening competition, deregulations encouraged the greed factor (please see chapter 3 for a detailed discussion of this concept). Perhaps the most important damage the deregulation movement caused is the counteracting of the principle of "any attempt to reduce competition or create monopoly power is illegal." This was the core value that the market economy was based on and with deregulation it lost its effectiveness almost completely. Thus, lawlessness created a reinforcement of the law of the jungle, meaning surviving through financial power.

Tax Cuts

A progressive income tax eliminates economic inequality and levels the playing field by creating almost equal opportunity as the key of economic activity. It started with John F. Kennedy considering the reduction in income tax rates to be a stimulator of economic growth. Having very few millionaires, at the time, Kennedy's tax reduction policy gave the people immediately increased purchasing power, which is a critical factor to combat a recession (see chapter 7). Kennedy was starting with the remnants of the recession that the previous administration was experiencing. However, tax reduction became the key principle of the Republican Party even though tax rates moved down from 92 percent to about 36 percent. The very rich in our society, that is, the 1 percenters, would want more. Flattening of the income tax, by definition, creates more economic inequality and takes away the possibility of having a leveled playing field for the population.

Deregulation combined with tax cuts encouraged outsourcing. Many well-paying American jobs went to India, China, or Mexico among others. Outsourcing of well-paying jobs is still continuing. Perhaps one of the most critical aspects of outsourcing is that as companies outsourced employment they closed their American factories. Even if they did not close down the US factory they put all of their efforts to establishing a most modern factory, say in China; thus, the American factories were not, and are not, able to compete with the advancing technology simply because of being ignored and not being updated. Similarly, as good jobs are being sent overseas the domestic education budgets are being reduced. Since domestic qualified workers are not as much in demand as before, the decline on education budgets has become routine. Emphasis on education for creating a more knowledgeable and capable labor force has lost its desirability.

Up until the early 1980s US mergers and acquisitions were in the form of buying out a failing enterprise and working with them so that they become productive and functional again. With the deregulationary movement and emergence of finance economy private equity finance companies emerged. Their main goal was not to make the failing company functional but to make as much money as possible by buying out companies by cutting down or eliminating their retirement programs, outsourcing their major functions, and receiving additional financial support from the American government. Their functions did not appear to be beneficial to the economy as a whole.

Merger Mania

Deregulation and tax breaks created a merger mania in the American economy, which is still going strong. Instead of competing, financial giants bought out newly emerging competition that made them look more profitable while they eliminated the competition. This had three major negative results. First, merger mania took away, at least partially, American competitiveness and innovativeness. Stronger and promising companies were bought out by financial giants and if these promising companies were direct competition for the financial giants they were stopped from being a threat to the giants. Thus, the prospect of creating radical innovations and being ahead of global competition deteriorated and American competitiveness declined.

Second, merger mania did not have much to do about companies becoming too big to fail. There were, and are, no size issues and this led to the creation of oligopolies, which further reduced competition and made the oligopolists very rich as their economic might has been used to increase profitability at any cost without considering the society's well-being and future advancement possibilities of the economy.

Third, the conditions created by merger mania discouraged younger companies, which may have had great future or at least positive future possibilities. This dampened the entrepreneurial spirit. Thus, merger mania first created the conditions and allowed major companies to merge. It further allowed some companies to reach the point of being too big to fail or too big to succeed. Many companies reached this particular point and because of the economic conditions they are in a reasonable shape financially, but they may be causing major damage to the economy's growth possibilities.

In 2001 I pointed out that the prevailing derailment of the economy is causing American consumers many major problems (Samli 2001). This was many billions of dollars of merger mania ago. Today it is no longer the American economy that is being derailed. It already has derailed to become a finance economy, which is financially manipulated from the top by some of the 1 percenters. There are no displayed concerns for consumers' well-being or the growth of the economy. The concerns for consumer well-being and progress of the economy as a whole are replaced by the finance economy where only a few are trying to gain as much financial advantage as possible. As a result, we have observed a major movement toward oligopolization of the economy with tremendous financial pressures to be controlled. This pattern has been continuing and, if anything, getting even stronger. This process is creating numerous problems for the American consumer as well as the American economy.

Problems Created for Consumers

In 2001 I listed a number of problems; in 2012, at the writing of this book, none of these problems have gone away, and, in fact, numerous others have emerged, as has been stated in many parts of this book. These conditions are not creating a situation of sustainability for the American economy. The proposed list is not complete and a number of other problems may be included.

- Americans are buying most of their basic necessities from China, India, Mexico, and so on. The outsourcing is making a few companies extremely rich while it is exporting American jobs to countries with lower labor costs.
- Americans are paying more for lesser quality services. Because of the less-than-adequate competition and some degree of poor communication in the economy, Americans are paying more for insurance, as credit card interest, and many other services. Again the conditions are very favorable for the finance groups.
- Americans are allowing a runaway banking system that is using their money, paying almost no interest, and charging them exorbitant fees. Furthermore, the banking system is getting involved in questionable and risky transactions with consumers' money.
- Americans, prior to the implementation of Obama care provisions, were trapped in a medical system where they were constantly paying more for fewer services.
- With the exception of top executives of financial giants and other 1 percenters, Americans are not holding their own. Job security is almost nonexistent, raises and advancements are not even present, retirement programs are in jeopardy, cost of education is becoming out of reach, and many Americans are paying more for their houses than their market value. Indeed many Americans are facing very serious problems, which are mostly working for the benefit of the financial sector. It appears that all of the conditions presented here are working against the American middle class and lower middle class. As the American middle class is shrinking the American lower class is expanding. Exhibit 2.2 illustrates the key factors causing, and the result of, this overall situation. Once again, this general pattern in the American economy is not sustainable.

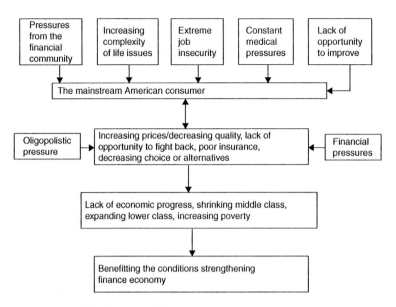

Exhibit 2.2   The dilemma of the American consumer.

The Dilemma of the Mainstream American Consumer

As can be seen from exhibit 2.2, the dilemma that American consumers are facing is caused by a number of underlying, far reaching, long-lasting, and unsustainable factors. Each point in the exhibit must be explored further. Many of them are discussed in different sections of this book.

The exhibit illustrates that as pressures generated by the financial community and other 1 percenters become more powerful the complexity of life issues is accelerating. Meeting the ends has become very difficult; job insecurity is making this situation much worse. Medical pressures, particularly before Obama care, have been tremendous and, perhaps above all, the lack of opportunities to fight off this total discouraging situation is playing havoc with the mainstream American consumers. The results of these negative forces are even more discouraging. They are pulling down the American economy except the 1 percenters.

As exhibit 2.2 illustrates, prices are increasing and the overall quality of all aspects of life appears to be decreasing. There are no alternatives to fight back except to display disapproval by perhaps votes and the occupation movement in many cities, which are put down by the police. Insurance companies based on lack of regulations are improving their financial positions despite the economic decline and disappearing of the middle class.

Exhibit 2.2 draws a gloomy picture indicating the lack of economic progress, middle-class shrinkage, and the expansion of poverty in the society. Unfortunately, all of these conditions are mainly outcomes of the functions of the finance economy. The whole process is going in the direction of decreased competition in favor of expanding extremely rich and gigantic oligopolies, which are constantly taking the American economy away from market conditions to a financial autocracy controlled and manipulated from the top, very similar to as described in story books misdeeds of evil kings. This financial control of the society cannot be justified when the democratic goals of the American society are considered. Those goals are totally dormant at this point.

More on the Road to Oligopolies

Just what happens, for instance, when two greatest banks merge? Let us explore the case of Wells Fargo, which bought out Wachovia. First of all, each bank has different customer policies and when the two combine some people will certainly be caught unaware, particularly when they receive pink slips. In such mergers, by definition, many are laid off. Here it must be emphasized that banking is a people business. People need choices as to where to bank and even how to bank. That choice is reduced. Much of the time consumers need people in the bank to talk to and to conduct business. But Wells Fargo in order to pay for the deal had cut out many thousand jobs. The clientele of the people who were laid off will be somewhat lost if they have been dealing with the same person for a long time. When the spokesperson for the bank stated that this move would add momentum and focus on serving their customers better, he/she was not being sincere. Certainly when a merger of this kind takes place hundreds or thousands of commercial credit centers and branches across the country are closed, which certainly reduces the choice of their customers. As early as 1998 Perman showed that after just about every bank merger there has been a reduction in services and increase in fees. Finally, and most importantly, as a result of all mergers, not the stakeholders (consumers and the society as a whole), but only some of the administrators are likely to benefit. Small companies, in these cases, argue that their very large rivals use extremely aggressive strategies to kill the competition coming from their small rivals. Such strategies are discussed in my earlier book (Samli 2001). As described in this case, companies eliminate competition through mergers and acquisitions and they become more oligopolistic and subsequently even monopolistic. Having a few firms controlling most of that particular industry, oligopoly, is different from only one company, a monopolist, controlling the industry. However, both of these situations are much different than a situation where many firms are competing and trying to be better than others, which would be the case in a market economy. However, oligopolistic tendencies of mergers have been and are very widespread. They are reducing competition to benefit the financial giants. In the absence of proper regulations, merger mania has been and is creating oligopolies.

Oligopolies Are Dinosaurs

Oligopolies are very large firms controlling much of an industry and do not compete in the traditional manner. They are not interested in being engaged in a price competition that should help the ultimate consumer. Oligopolists are worried about price wars in which they all lose. Thus, they avoid one-upmanship on prices. In the meantime they also develop a series of problems.

- Poor flexibility
- Weak market sensitivity
- Lack of satisfactory R&D
- Questionable core competency
- Effectiveness issue

Exhibit 2.3   Special problems of oligopolies.

Exhibit 2.3 presents five such key problems. These are related to flexibility, market sensitivity, R&D activity, core competencies, and overall effectiveness. These are closely related to the conditions that too-big-to-failers display.

Poor flexibility: As part of being too big to fail or too big to succeed, American oligopolists are so gigantic that it makes them inflexible. It takes much time to respond to an unexpected market problem. In fact, most of the time they simply cannot respond. They may not even detect some of the major changes in the economy until it is very late.

Weak market sensitivity: If consumers do not have many viable options, they cannot switch; therefore, they cannot make good decisions. Buying out the competition, by definition, eliminates consumer options and hence diminishes the possibilities for consumers to switch to other brands or change businesses or services they currently are using. If consumers do not have many options there is no progress. In oligopolies the business does not feel the necessity to be sensitive to consumer needs, since consumers have no place to go. These large oligopolists who have captured large portions of the industry do not feel the need to improve and to be more responsive to consumer needs or enhance their own sensitivity to predict the forthcoming needs of the consuming public. One very critical and related area needs to be discussed further here, that is, as mergers take place, many well-paying middle management jobs are also eliminated. And furthermore many others are reduced both in numbers and in pay. This combined with the fact that the finance economy does not create good-quality, high-paying jobs makes the whole society poorer.

Lack of satisfactory R&D: When a giant company has a large portion of the industry and a good cash position, it does not feel any obligation to explore the unknown and commit large resources on research and development (R&D). In such cases, large size interferes with society's opportunities to reach out and develop better products and services. Furthermore, companies that are extensively involved in merger mania put most of their resources into the merger-related areas that limit their R&D resources and hence they stay away from risky basic research and costly R&D projects. Most giant corporations have top managements who need to have high profiles for the public and need to show profits in the short run. Since R&D is mainly a longer term proposition, they are not very interested in R&D related services (Porter 1990).

Questionable core competency: Firms, in general, have a certain core competency area in which they excel. These competency areas are their bread and butter and help maintain their existence. Much of the time, mergers, acquisitions, and unfriendly takeovers complicate the picture. Who has major core competency and who has administrative power becomes a problem? Furthermore, as merger mania continues, it becomes critical to decide what the firm's core competencies are and if the people with proper background are controlling these positions. Sometimes merger mania will create a confusion about the key focus of the firm. The case of Sears is an example. After having been the number one merchandiser for over half a century, Sears got engaged in big time diversification. It got into banking, real estate insurance, and other major financial activities to a point where it lost its focus and got away from its core competency areas. Sears lost large amounts of money and its market position. When such situations occur, both the company and the society lose much.

Effectiveness issue: It is very difficult to claim an increased effectiveness as companies continue their merger acquisition activities and become oligopolists. In merger situations if the two companies have the same core competencies the merger activity would reduce many of the high-paying jobs since the new company does not need duplication. If the core competencies of the newly merging companies are different, then the new core competency becomes a question mark and perhaps both companies lose ground. One further observation is that as the mergers continue fewer and fewer companies control the industry. In such cases firms begin emphasizing or imitators of their competitor's behaviors and the progressiveness of the society suffers (Bennett 1998; Perman 1998). Thus, oligopolistic tendencies are a historic activity and have no place in modern dynamic societies.

Summary

This chapter analyzes just how the market economy has been replaced by the finance economy. First, a discussion of three major trends—deregulation, tax cuts, and merger mania—is presented. As these three trends continue, the finance economy becomes stronger. This is partially due to the tendency of creating oligopolies.

Oligopolistic tendencies can create too-big-to-fail type of companies, which are discussed in chapter 4. Oligopolies have about five special problem areas that are emphasized in this chapter. These are: poor flexibility, weak market sensitivity, lack of satisfactory R&D, questionable core competency, and effectiveness of oligopolists. In all cases the society is the loser.

Chapter 3

Greed, the Unfortunate Financial Disease

Unfortunately, the 1 percent financiers in our society are suffering from a disease I call "greed." This is an insidious disease that is not well recognized. The 1 percent of the people in our society are more interested in simply making more money any way they can without any consideration for the society and its future. They emphasize financial values over human values.

This chapter posits that capitalism goes in two different directions: encouraging ambition or encouraging greed. It is also maintained that unchecked ambition in time becomes greed. While the ambitious are constructive people—they innovate, create jobs, and are givers to the society—the greedy consider only their own financial benefits—they block progress if it is not in their favor and are takers. In this chapter, first the orientations of the greedy versus the ambitious are contrasted. Then some key practices of the greedy and the ambitious are explored. Finally, different orientations to curb greed and therefore support ambition are examined. It is emphasized here that while greed may almost destroy our society and the prevailing quality of life, ambition would create economic progress and enhancement of the quality of life. Perhaps above all it must be recognized that if and when ambition becomes greed, the American society moves away from being a market economy and a finance economy takes over. This is an extremely dangerous development.

When Schumpeter (1934) called innovation as "creative destruction" he certainly did not mean to support the recent concept of "vulture capitalism," which creates unemployment at the advancement of making money orientation and is the prevailing sentiment and practice in the current American economy. At the writing of this chapter about 350 families are estimated to own as much wealth as 150 million Americans. Ratigan (2012) discussed them as corporate vampires. Vampire industries and vampire companies prey on their customers:"[T]hey don't make money they just take it" (8). After all, capitalism is not just making money for a few privileged people or organizations; it is perceived to be a most important vehicle to advance the society and to make it more prosperous for all. But, this original orientation toward the market system is no longer in existence. The 1 percenters have been trying to change it and they seem to be succeeding.

At the writing of this book millions of Americans are complaining that 99 percent of the society is working for the remaining 1 percent. Indeed between 1979 and 2007 the earnings of the upper 1 percent increased by 275 percent, the income of the middle-income group of 60 percent increased by only 40 percent, and the income of the lowest fifth of our society increased by only 18 percent (CBO 2011).

This situation is described as the financial crises in the American economy. I would call it the "blooming greed factor." Hansen and Movahedi (2010) explain the current financial situation that created the deepest recession of recent history. This recession started with a housing bubble, which became extremely dangerous. It almost sent the American financial sector into total bankruptcy and created a very widespread unemployment picture.

Perhaps in order to understand this complex and extremely alarming situation, it may be important to make a distinction between individual motivational issues and organizational structures (Marx 1967). These two interacted and reinforced each other toward the advancement of the society. However, in our advanced industrial society these two layers of behaviors are becoming comingled with a very negative pattern challenging the industrial foundations of our society. Unfortunately, a very small group of multimillionaires have become extremely powerful and are controlling the society in such a way that their economic well-being is constantly improving as more and more Americans are becoming poor. One estimation in this regard is that CEOs were making 25–30 times more than the average labor wages around 1988. By 2000 this ratio had become 350 times and it is increasing nonstop (Reich 2007). These people are still asking for more tax breaks even though they do not show any positive performance in job creation or great contribution to economic progress despite the nonstop propaganda.

From Ambition to Greed

Ideally capitalism "allows individuals to choose how they allocate their time where (and if) they work and what to do with their money they earn" (Hicks 2004). These were very important motivations for individual entrepreneurs at the earlier stages of modern American capitalism. Ambitious and entrepreneurial people developed the industrial fabric of our country. They were hardworking and always anxious to get better and to do more. They created employment and economic wealth. Unfortunately, as small firms became industrial giants, the individuals who were at the top of these industrial giants became greedy rather than ambitious. Their egotistic pursuits of self-interest created insatiable passions and appetites for more financial power (Durkheim 1951; Hansen and Movahedi 2010). Marx (1967) termed this behavior as "boundless greed after riches." While Rand and Boesky maintained greed is good (Boesky 1985; Hicks 2004), they did not distinguish between ambition and greed. Samli (2010) stated that the twenty-first-century capitalism with its free-wheeling, with no enforcement of any authority, with tremendously powerful self-interest, and with lacking consideration for the society as a whole is gaining more power at the expense of the workers, the poor, and the elderly. Certain select CEOs and corporate entities are behaving as if the society's economic well-being is a zero-sum game, which means that blind selfishness will emasculate the possibilities of a fair and widespread economic growth (Wachtel 2003). When the economy is described as a zero-sum game, then the assumption is that in order to advance some other people's wealth must be confiscated.

"Whereas the ambition factor is reasonably constructive and rewarding both to the individual and the society, the greed factor, although possibly very lucrative to certain individuals, can be and in most cases is extremely destructive to the society." It is even more so globally, since stakes are greater and controls are even weaker in the global picture (Samli 2010, 10).

In order to check and, it is hoped, stop the greed factor it is necessary to understand its orientation and practices.

A Comparative Analysis of Greed versus Ambition

Understanding the greed factor is articulated by contrasting it with the ambition factor. Exhibit 3.1 puts forth such an effort. The two concepts are analyzed and contrasted on the basis of eight key points of analysis. These are: constructive atmosphere, perception of the world, personality traits, time dimension, civic-mindedness, selfishness element, accomplishment goals, and attitude toward performance.

The greed factor displays itself in the form of a "get them before they get you mentality." It drives individuals to win in any way, shape, or form. It brings about the feeling that one's advancement depends on just how many people one can walk over.

The ambition factor on the other hand, generates the feeling that working and collaborating with other people enhances opportunities for progress. In other words it enhances entrepreneurial orientation. Here the understanding is that there is room for advancement not only for one percent at the expense of all others, but there is room for

Greed Factor		Ambition Factor
	Constructive atmosphere	
Get them before they get you. Win any way you can, step on as many bodies as needed		Working and collaborating with people. There are opportunities for everyone
	Perception of the world	
Get as much as you can at any cost. You cannot change the world. Exploit it		There could be much progress through cooperation and mutual advancement
	Personality traits	
Mean, grabbing, I got mine you do whatever you do as long as you don't stand in my way orientation		Generous, sharing knowledge and opportunity. Working with others and allowing others to raise themselves by way of orientation
	Time dimension	
What do I want? Everything. When do I want them now? There is no time		There is time for improvement and advancement. We can wait as long as there is progress
	Civic mindedness	
I don't care about the environment. I don't care about the poor. My well-being is critical		If the environment is improved, if the poor have more money we will be better off
	Selfishness element	
Must get all that I can for the number one (me). There should not be any limits		There is enough talent for progress. If the society was better, we all benefit
	Accomplishment goals	
Get as much as I can, let the world take care of itself		See if I could make a success of this undertaking; can I hire more people? Can I expand my business?
	Attitude toward performance	
Assumes all was done by themselves		Appreciates all the help that was given for the accomplishments

Exhibit 3.1 Contrasting the orientation of the greedy versus the ambitious.
Source: Adapted and revised from Samli (2013).

progress and opportunity for all. That is a constructive orientation, which unfortunately has been lost.

In terms of the perception of the world the greed factor moves in the direction of getting everything one can possibly get. The world is there and getting anything basically means taking things away from others. Since the world is developed, our advancement will be based on others' loss.

However, the ambition factor generates the feeling that working and collaborating with other people enhances opportunities for progress on a large-scale basis. Here it must be reiterated that not one percenters but the whole society must advance.

Thus, in term of the perception of the world the greed factor does not consider other alternatives but just get everything that you possibly can get. Since the world is already developed, getting things basically means taking things away from others which is the zero-sum game orientation. In a developed world advancement is based on others' loss.

The ambition factor, on the other hand, advocates that there is much progress that can be made and that progress can be very good for all participants. The world can be changed and improved. All people can benefit from such change and improvement.

The personality traits of those under the spell of the greed factor include selfishness and meanness. They think in terms of "I am going to get mine whatever it takes and nobody should stand in my way." Again, people who are motivated by the ambition factor have different personality traits. They are generous, knowledge sharing, and forward looking about existing and potential opportunities. They work cooperatively with others and let others also advance as they advance themselves. They believe success is created jointly, not individually.

The time dimension for the greed factor followers is now. They want everything and they want it now. There is no time to waste and, therefore, it should not be wasted. Ambitious people, on the other hand, realize that there is time for improvement. In fact, good performance and advancement take time. They are willing to wait as long as there is progress. There is enough time for everything.

Civic mindedness of the greed factor group involves the thought that paying any attention to the environment is hardly profitable, so why bother. They see environmental efforts as costly and unnecessary. Their general orientation is "I don't care about pollution, nor do I care about the poor or the elderly. I must make as much money as possible." The ambitious group takes the position that if the environment is improved and if the poor and elderly are cared for, there will be more money and, as a result, more jobs and more benefits for everyone. The poor and the elderly will buy their products or services, which will further stimulate the whole economy.

The greedy express selfishness by saying that "I must get all what I can for number one (me) and this should not have any limits and barriers." This is basically their goal. Whatever happens to other people is not a problem for the greedy. The ambitious element, however, considers the fact that there is much talent out there and that the whole society will benefit from the utilization of this talent. Progress is teamwork and working with others is synergistic (Samli 2010). In terms of accomplishments the greed factor, once again, emphasizes self-advancement. It is totally immune to the world and to the condition of others. The ambition factor makes people think how they could make their activities successful so that more people would benefit.

Greed factor claims that accomplishments are totally self-made. The dominant thinking here is that "I did it all by myself." The ambition factor makes people more appreciative of all the help they can get. The assumption of course is that it takes many people's efforts to accomplish positive and successful ventures.

Although exhibit 3.1 illustrates two extreme pictures of greed and ambition, it must be recognized that at one point there may be only a fine line between the two. It is certainly reasonable to believe that all human beings can be ambitious but this ambition could easily turn into an extreme level of greed. This point indicates that there is a necessity of having ambition checked and the greed possibilities need to be blocked. Ambition may reach a point of great success, which could easily turn into greed. As once stated brilliantly, power corrupts, and absolute power corrupts absolutely.

When Bill Gates developed the preliminaries of windows in a dorm room, it was ambition. However, subsequently, some courts both in the United States and in Europe have claimed that Microsoft started using its power in an abusive manner and has been exercising a stifling monopoly over competition and competitors. Thus, ambition has become greed. But, it must be understood that the greedy and the ambitious have quite different modus operandi.

Differences in the Practices

Exhibit 3.2 illustrates the critical contradictions between the practices of the greedy and that of the ambitious. As can be seen, the ambition factor can be very constructive for the future and for economic progress; the greed factor creates a larger gap between haves and have-nots.

The greedy try to minimize or eliminate competition by mergers or acquisitions; the ambitious increase competition and employment by expansion. From this perspective it may easily be said that greed is the enemy of ambition. Ambitious and successful newly emerging small businesses or entrepreneurs are being gobbled up by greedy corporate pirates.

The greedy limit the pay of subordinates, thinking that there will be more remaining for them. The ambitious, on the other hand, hope to generate a better distribution of income so that the markets will also be greater and that would be beneficial to the society.

The greedy will outsource only to lower costs so that there will be more profit for them. The ambitious will outsource to improve quality and to create more participation of others so that there will be a more even distribution of benefits for all and therefore a consumer surplus in time.

The greedy will use their economic powers to receive unfair and excessive favors from the existing political establishments at the loss of the whole society. The ambitious will be engaged in spreading the power base as much as possible so that the poor and

Practices of the Greedy	Practices of the Ambitious
Likes to expand by buying out competition or by generating competition-reducing mergers	Likes to expand by starting new plants or new businesses and create more employment
Blocks increases in minimum wages. Gives unrealistic raises to those who are very rich and powerful	Supports better distribution of income and results of economic progress for all
Outsources not to improve quality but to maximize profits that go to the top management only	Outsources to improve quality and to solicit participation of others
Uses its power to receive greater favors from political bodies	Emphasizes spreading the power base to as many as possible
Does not share proceeds with those who contribute much to the profitability	Shares proceeds with all who contributed to work as proportionately as possible

Exhibit 3.2   Shocking differences in modus operandi.
Source: Adapted and revised from Samli (2013).

underprivileged would enjoy equal opportunities and the society would advance.

The greedy will not share the profits with those who help them to generate those profits. The ambitious will consider the contribution of the entire group of participants in the economic activity in proportion to their participation and their contribution. This will create even greater profits in the future to be shared equitably. It will also help the markets to expand and the economy to grow.

At this point it becomes obvious that the society will go backward if the greedy can have their way. During the past decade or so the extraordinary efforts in the United States to privatize and deregulate have already caused a tremendous discrepancy between the economic well-being of the top 1 percent of the income category and the rest of the society. This is a dangerous trend as is reiterated many times in this book. According to some mass media reporting about 7 of the richest people of the country have greater economic well-being than about 98 million Americans.

This could get even worse if some corrective action does not take place.

Destructive Practices of the Greedy

Exhibit 3.3 illustrates some of the most destructive practices of the greedy. Although the practices listed are well known and do not need to be discussed individually, the following needs to be emphasized.

Laying off workers in recessions has become almost a common practice of global giants. They try to maintain their profit levels by cutting labor costs rather than, perhaps, accelerating their proactive marketing activities to generate new revenues. They are what Ratigan (2012) calls capitalists who take rather than capitalist type of businesses who give. The capitalists that take are sucking-up the blood of our industrial system (Ratigan 2012).

Perhaps part of the major destructive activity is being engaged in union busting (Reich, 2007). If the thinking is that the size of the pizza is fixed, then trying to get a larger slice of it would involve not paying as much to labor. How do you accomplish that? Of course by union busting. Union busting, at the writing of this book, is going more forcefully than ever before.

- Laying off workers in recessions to maintain profits
- Vulture capitalism, buying out companies that are struggling and putting them out of existence for large returns
- Union busting to take away bargaining positions of labor so that they will pay less to workers
- Exercising merger mania to limit competition
- Blocking off developments of disruptive technologies so that they will get more for their investments
- Influencing politicians to maintain low tax rates
- Charging exorbitant penalties for delayed loan payments
- Reducing salaries and requiring more work of labor

Exhibit 3.3   Some of the key destructive practices of the greedy leading to the strengthening of a finance economy.
Source: Adapted and revised from Samli (2013).

Again, if it is assumed that the size of a pizza pie, or profit picture in this case, is fixed, eliminating possible competition is a major activity, which is achieved through merger mania. This activity has been going on in our society since about the early 1980s (Samli 2001). The same argument goes for radical innovations created by disruptive technologies. The alternative energy explorations, for instance, have been blocked by the petroleum lobby in our society. It is very profitable for petroleum companies to do what they have been doing, regardless of how damaging that could be, rather than allowing cheaper, environmentally friendly, and renewable energy to be developed.

There is no doubt that availability of money, rather than the well-being and the future of our society is controlling national economic decisions approved or encouraged by the US Congress. As Ratigan (2012) posits the greedy are making fortunes by skimming money from the customers. This has been going on for a long while now.

Dual paycheck families are not a concept indicating ambition but are a response of the consumers to the squeezing forces exerted by the greedy. Dual paychecks are the result of reduced salaries imposed upon the workers in our society since about the early 1980s. The squeeze by the greedy is becoming more and more powerful and even dual paycheck families are not able to make ends meet.

Key Practices of the Ambitious

Exhibit 3.4 deals with this all-important topic. Above all, ambitious are the capitalists who make as opposed to those who take (Ratigan 2012).

They are typically supporters of major innovations and they create jobs. Not only do they hire more people, they also work very closely with them and give them credit for what they do.

The ambitious work with labor groups and recognize the importance of labor in their progress. Rewarding work is one of the most

- Starting new businesses and being entrepreneurial and creating jobs
- Being partially or fully responsible for innovations and encouraging their advancements
- Hiring more people and working closely with them
- Giving credit for the work associates do and sharing the benefits of business activities
- Working closely with the unions or labor groups
- Rewarding work equitable to what associates perform
- In recessions, not laying off people but bearing the burden equitably
- Supporting disruptive technologies as much as possible

Exhibit 3.4   How do the ambitious contribute.
Source: Adapted and revised from Samli (2013).

important features of this group. They share the proceeds of the total activity.

As mentioned earlier they do not lay off people during difficult economic times, instead they bear the burden of a recession by sacrificing partially their own incomes if necessary.

Finally, this group is not attached to existing technologies. They look for new ideas and new ways; therefore, they support disruptive technologies and radical innovations (Samli 2008); in short, they are entrepreneurial.

Deadly Sins and the Greedy

Some years ago Peter Drucker (1995) pointed out that there are five deadly sins that businesses commit. What is surprising and perhaps alarming is the fact that all of these five sins contribute to the short-run money-making activity even though in the long run they are not only dangerous for the business but are almost deadly for the society. Perhaps the most unfortunate part of these sins is that they describe the behavior of the greedy. Exhibit 3.5 describes these five deadly sins. As can be seen, the first sin deals with worshipping high profit, which is already discussed in this chapter. It means I will make as much as I can make in the short run, the society and even

Sins	Impact
Worshipping high profit	Charging exorbitant prices may destroy the firm's demand and exploit those who have no alternatives
Charging the maximum prices the market can bear	Extremely risky for the business in the long run, enhances financial gains unnecessarily in the short run
Pricing products based on cost-plus	Again, in the short run this practice brings in a lot of money but in the long run the economy suffers
Slaughtering tomorrow	The aforementioned three sins implies that greed does not have a tomorrow
Feeding problems and starving opportunities	The money-making schemes in the short run do not allow one to think of the opportunities in the long run

Exhibit 3.5   Deadly sins and their impact.

the world are not important to me. The second sin is connected to the first; it basically says, "I will get as much as I possibly can right now." The third sin also connected to the first two in the sense that the greedy will cover all of the costs immediately and charge an exorbitant profit margin on top of that cost. The fourth sin as already implied is the fact "let tomorrow take care of itself I am doing business today." Finally, the fifth sin, which is more damaging and most regressive, is that "I am doing what I do well now and I do not care for other possible and beneficial opportunities." This orientation, of course, blocks innovations and future progress.

The author believes that those greedy groups that are at the top are major corporate entities that practice this way. They constantly commit the five deadly sins.

Greed, in Fact, May Backfire in Time

It has been stated that Steve Jobs, the innovator and founder of Apple, had declared war on "copycats" before he died. At the top of copycats list is Samsung, the Korean giant that received $8 billion worth of orders from Apple. The way it is set up Apple's Ipad and Iphone operations would come to a total halt without Samsung parts. Originally, Apple shared patents with Samsung, which was a company capable of producing certain parts for Apple products giving Apple a big short-run profitability. But now Apple is suing Samsung for flooding the market with copycat products. Samsung's website lists about 134 phone models and Apple has had only 2. In fact, the copycat activities have been expanding both in Europe as well as in the United States. In the meantime, Samsung shipped 36 million smart phones all over the world. Thus, Apple has numerous lawsuits against copycats and thus far it has paid over $400 million in legal fees without being able to stop their action.

It must be noted that if Apple was less greedy and more patient at the beginning, it could have started a number of factories with $400 million and also created thousands of American jobs. But above all it could have made much more money.

Combatting Greed

Without harming individual freedoms and positive economic initiatives, it is extremely important that the greed factor be checked. There are at least three general areas that need to be considered in counteracting greed: ethical, legal, and financial. Additional comments are added on this topic at the end of this book.

Ethical countergreed: Perhaps this movement started earlier than the legal and financial considerations. This idea may be supported by the increasing courses in the business curricula during the past decade or so. It is only hoped that these courses are primarily supporting ambition and condemning greed, but it is not definite that this is what is happening. By definition, these courses can make a strong case for ambition, which certainly is critically needed in our society. It is necessary for business ethics courses to consider the greed-versus-ambition issues with the hopes that articulating ambition for the common good will overpower greed.

Legal countergreed: Any attempt to create monopoly power or reduce competition must be outlawed. Although this sentiment has been articulated by antitrust laws for a long time now, it certainly has not been enforced forcefully. Since the early 1980s this country has been plagued by merger mania, which, by definition, creates monopoly power or reduces competition in the market. This pattern has not stopped and many major industries have become one step closer to being oligopolies. In addition, limiting competition oligopolies create tremendous discrepancies in income distribution. This point was implied by J. K. Galbraith as early as 1956; subsequently many authors reasserted the same point (Samli 2001). Invariably, oligopolistic tendencies lead in the direction of the greed factor. Leaders of oligopolistic firms become extremely rich and powerful and, as stated earlier, rather ruthless and greedy. An extreme example is that of Enron, a company that put individuals at risk for health-related illness and death by instigating illegal and unfair manipulation of electric power in California (Hansen and Movahedi 2010). Perhaps most of the white-collar crimes are the result of the greed factor, which resulted due to lack of legal constraints. If the greed factor is allowed to proceed unchecked the government sooner or later will be forced to regulate and even overregulate (Barton 2011). However, the greed factor, at the writing of this book, needs to be regulated so that the American capitalism will have a future and the American economy will go back to being market oriented.

Financial countergreed: Greed basically receives its power and is based on financial resources and financial gains. Obviously, if it were decided that greed needs to be somewhat curbed, it will have to be curbed primarily financially. This financial curbing may have at least three prongs to be considered: income, capital, and sharing of resources. Here income includes resources that are used to meet immediate needs. Capital is unused income converted into different types of stockpiling that generates further market power (Hill and Cassill 2004). The sharing of resources is the third prong of the financial control considerations; it is considered to be an investment of group capital to enhance individual survival in the community or the society (Hill and Cassill 2004). It is obvious that each of these three prongs need to be studied and dealt with in detail one at a time and then all three considered together. Suffice it to say here that through regulations and taxation laws the acquisition and distribution of income, capital, and resources need to be arranged so that the ambition factor will be supported and the greed factor is closely controlled. This, however, is not happening in our very questionable climate.

Summary

This chapter deals with perhaps one of the most critical and misunderstood social issues, termed by this author as the "greed factor," and it is a great danger to our society. It must be understood that left alone ambition could become greed and the benefits of ambition, which could move a society into a progressive economic state, could be totally stopped and the society could become regressive. Some thinkers propose that in time natural selection will shape the rules of both greed and sharing into certain patterns of behavior (Hill and Cassill 2004). If such behaviors operationalize the corporations' mission, values, goals, and objectives would operationalize the acquisition and distribution of income and resources. In the twenty-first century superdynamic societal and managerial conditions may either take a dangerously long time to make conditions beneficial for all or those conditions may never materialize. In fact, this chapter indicates that when ambition becomes greed, then the market economy, which was, and is, the foundation of American progress, is changed into a finance economy, which does not perform for the society as a whole.

NOTE: This chapter is a revised version of my earlier chapter titled "The Greed Factor," which appeared in Economics of Competition by Nova Publishers. Editors are: Georg Leismuller and Elias J. Schimpf.

Chapter 4

Too Big to Fail or Too Big to Succeed

There is an optimality issue with all functional activities. In businesses the optimality is related to size. It maybe stated that there is an optimal size for all organizations.

As the American economy became more and more finance directed, numerous corporate giants became more and more gigantic. As companies emerge at the entrepreneurial level they are more people oriented in the market and survive in their people orientations. However, as they grow and become powerhouses, of course only a few, they become more and more self-oriented once again; as stated earlier they move from being ambitious to being greedy. Greed in this case makes them bigger, more powerful, and basically less caring of the people and the society as a whole. British Petroleum digs much deeper in the beaches of Louisiana, even though not equipped to go that far, and creates an unbelievable environmental disaster. Toyota has been trying to accept a problem of uncontrollable acceleration in its about eight million cars. Gigantic banks approved selling homes to millions of unqualified customers and created first a housing bubble and then the deepest recession in the United States since the Great Depression. Financial power in the absence of regulation and directed by greed goes well beyond the benefits and progressiveness of market economies. The worst thing perhaps is that these corporate giants are very independent and nonsharing of economic rewards when the economy is in good shape, but they become "socialistic" and ask for government help when the economy reaches a deep recession situation. Then the concept of "too big to fail" becomes a major concept and the federal government helps them at the expense of the society as a whole. This concept of too big to fail raises its ugly head every time a recession reaches a point where the cost to consumers becomes extremely high. In early 1990s the savings and loan fiasco cost the consumers hundreds of billions of dollars, and in 2007 the financial housing bubble is still costing unbelievable sums to ultimate consumers and to the American society as a whole. Ratigan (2012) used a very interesting term. He called these mega companies "trillion dollar vampires." After 2008, the US Congress considered the problems created by their practices in the banking sector and seized on the crises to meddle in banks, in their credit card dealings, their fees, and other details that can be swept under the title of "reform and consumer protection." This was done to end the concept of too-big-to-fail to no avail. Since 2008, big banks have gotten bigger and once again they are counteracting the new regulations, which were designed to prevent another financial disaster (Dodd 2012).

Just How Big Is Too Big?

Stern and Feldman (2004) have written about the bank bailout as an evidence of the dangers of being too big to fail. One of the most critical issues in dealing with this all-important topic is determining how big too-big-to-fail is. Perhaps by the time a greedy giant reaches the point of too-big-to-fail, it is much too late. George Romney, the president of an auto manufacturing company smaller than GM, maintained at one point that GM was just too big to be managed efficiently. But since then the company got much bigger and became a too-big-to-fail type of an institution. Although it got rescued and is functioning reasonably well the major question is whether or not the company is too big to succeed. The company has grown into a complex and diversified global enterprise complex that has accumulated too much cost and perhaps even more importantly there is too much size to be managed efficiently (Taleb and Tapiero 2010). This is true for thousands of companies that are at this particular stage.

Key Problems of Being Oversized

Exhibit 4.1 illustrates seven groups of problems that need to be carefully explored. These seven groups of problems are related to the markets, practices, commitments, technology, the economy, personalities, and innovation. It must be emphasized that in the current finance economy these issues are not carefully explored.

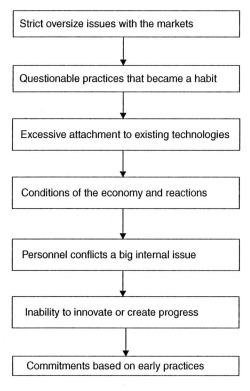

Strict oversize issues with the markets

Questionable practices that became a habit

Excessive attachment to existing technologies

Conditions of the economy and reactions

Personnel conflicts a big internal issue

Inability to innovate or create progress

Commitments based on early practices

Exhibit 4.1 The key problems of being oversized.

The Markets

When a company reaches a certain size it becomes not very profitable to deal with scattered and small market segments. This is where the 80–20 principle is discussed in businesses—80 percent of the income comes from about 20 percent of the customers. Thus, it may not be very profitable to deal with some of the customers in the 80 percent group. Furthermore, industrial giants become more and more isolated from their markets as they become too big. Also, as they are more and more isolated from their markets they do not readily comprehend the changes that may be taking place in their markets. Even if they become aware of certain new problems in their markets, the industrial giants cannot quickly create certain activities to cope with these problems because decision-making in certain size levels becomes much slower and burdensome.

Practices

Drucker (1995) brilliantly discussed five deadly business sins that typically become almost natural practices.

The first sin is the worship of high profit margins and of "premium pricing." This is almost totally natural in the finance-controlled markets.

The second sin is charging what the market will bear. Not only is it exploitative, it is also not a good competitive policy.

The third sin is cost-driven pricing. To begin with, this may be unrealistic because of size inefficiencies. It is also not a good approach because of it does not pay enough attention to consumer values.

The fourth sin according to Drucker is simply slaughtering tomorrow's opportunity on the altar of yesterday. This means not being aware of the changes in the market, which represent consumers' changing and perhaps more intensified needs.

Finally, the fifth sin that this author considers extremely important is feeding problems and starving opportunities. Instead of becoming more creative and innovative, many corporate giants simply deal with the problems at hand even though they may not be very critical. Similarly, as they may exaggerate and put much emphasis on existing problems they may be missing major opportunities in areas that they are not even exploring. Thus, they stop being progressive in a major way. The big-sized giants thus become less functional than what they used to be. These very large and powerful firms; however, they still have tremendous economic power. In a finance economy they are free to buy out new companies that may be progressive and perhaps more competitive and even put them out of existence.

The Commitments

Sull (2005) named certain practices as common traps. These traps, just as the previous section showed, interfere with the advancement and progressiveness of companies. As the companies in a finance-driven economy are allowed to become extremely gigantic they do not develop certain values, which is not necessarily good for the company, nor are they helpful to the economy. Their resources become millstones. For example, IBM for many years spent billions of dollars on hardware and software for the 360 computer lines. At the writing of this book, the largest bank JP Morgan and Chase has lost more than five billion dollars.

As the corporations become too big their processes become routines and they cannot quite get away from them. Compaq at one time being the innovation leader in the computer industry lost much because its processes became routines and it did not really cope with the upcoming new competition.

Again as the companies become very big, in time their relationships with customers, investors, governments, suppliers, and partners become extremely limiting and disrupt the progressive behaviors.

As financial growth and accumulation of power continues values become dogmas. Originally, preference for a sound set of values commands strong loyalties from employees and forges strong bonds with customers, attracts like-minded partners, and holds the company together. But again with time these values become dogmas and become all-encompassing, which creates a critical block for progress. Thus, the commitments and values in very large corporations become a burden to them as well as to the society. The next problem area, as shown in exhibit 4.1, is excessive attachment to existing technologies.

Too Much Emphasis on Existing Technologies

Christensen (2003) has pointed out that there are two types of innovations: radical and incremental. Radical innovations present much better products or even totally new products by using disruptive technologies. However, disruptive technologies are not favored and encouraged by the industrial giants who rely heavily on existing technologies even though they are not as productive as the newer ones. This is how silver halide photography, at a major loss to Kodak, has given way to digital photography. Similarly, wire line telephones are being replaced by mobile telephones, notebook computers are being replaced by hand-held digital appliances, and so on. This list can go on almost indefinitely. However, the key issue here is that as the companies become too big they have too much investment in the existing technologies and do not want to move in the direction of the radical technology support. This is not very good for the economy as a whole. Conditions of the economy create another group of harmful practices.

Conditions of the Economy

As corporate entities grow, in time their orientation changes—from being dynamic and small entrepreneurial entities to large, self-centered entities. Friedman (2010) distinguishes these two groups as start-ups versus bailouts. As a recession sets in start-ups will try to do more, will become more counter-recessionary by being more proactive. They will hire more people and be more aggressive in fighting the recession. On the other hand the bailouts who control the major portion of the financial economy immediately try to start laying off workers so that they maintain their financial powers. Thus they actually help recessions to get worse; they are a major drag on the economy.

Personnel Conflicts

This is perhaps the most important, least-known, and barely researched area, which this author considers to be the most critical burden on the economy. Exhibit 4.2 is constructed to explore this important but mainly ignored concept more carefully.

Personnel conflicts in gigantic financial companies may begin with a number of people having different pet projects. The project to be implemented or explored may be an important successful emotional victory in the organization rather than most promising and important area of exploration. Thus the pet project situation may not at all represent progress and true development.

Similarly, numerous high officials may be strongly committed to technological exploration. Once again, rather than employing most meritorious exploration may be totally ignored since it is not being championed by an important executive. Personality conflicts and individual dislikes may be extremely harmful since those who are in conflict may try to disregard or block others' ideas or projects. Thus progress may be replaced by strictly going backward. Finally, there

---

- Pet projects
- Strong commitments
- Excessive ambition
- Personality conflicts
- Maintaining the corporate status

Exhibit 4.2   Personnel conflicts.

may be certain groups working on different aspects of the organi-zational functions, but they may be in strong competition to obtain an important position in the corporate organization and gain more important status. All of these and perhaps other conflicts become unspecified but extremely disruptive. Needless to say personnel con-flicts are not likely to take place in dynamic entrepreneurial start-up companies. But they are extremely active and disruptive in gigantic bailout companies.

Innovation

As partially discussed in chapter 1, the lack of interest or motiva-tion on the part of financial giants to emphasize innovation is creat-ing a major handicap for the American economy. The 1 percenters lay emphasis on financial gains in the short run; however, emphasis on innovation, although very risky and costly, is a very profitable undertaking in the long run. The financial giants who are doing quite well in the short run are not motivated enough to spend much money on very risky long-term projects, which may not even pay off. Thus, they shy away from major, costly and risky research activity in the long run.

The Failure of Too-Big-to-Failers

The finance-driven economy since the 1980s has been favoring large size and monetary power with almost no regulation. The free mar-ket concept, although totally finance driven, has been reduced to the law of the jungle—survive and don't think or worry about the environment and the society.

It must be emphasized that first if they are too big to fail just what would it take to think that left alone they could succeed. This author believes that these two go hand in hand. Exhibit 4.3 brings about this major theme as the starting point. As discussed throughout this

- From being too big to fail to being too big to succeed
- Disrupting the economic progress
- Creating tremendous income inequalities

Exhibit 4.3 Too-big-to-failers' failures.

chapter, size can easily become a burden. But from a financial greed perspective, the more the financial power is the merrier it is. This orientation and the impact of the overgrown industrial giants are not helping but disrupting the economic progress the market-driven economy promised. The market-driven economy promised competition and not having excessive powers to disrupt competition. The finance-drive economy is in the process of creating oligopolies and finance-driven power rather than competition. The merger mania that started around the early 1980s has created nothing but overgrown companies thriving on tremendous income inequalities. In the market economy merger mania would have been stopped by antitrust laws. But these are not even questioned or acknowledged in the finance economy.

Summary

This chapter presents a very important discussion regarding the size of an organization being extremely important for its economic progress or lack thereof. Unfortunately, this issue is totally ignored in a finance-driven economy. There are at least seven groups of problem areas that need to be explored to decide if too-big-to-failers are also too big to succeed. These are: markets, practices, commitments, technology, the economy, personalities, and innovation. Just about all of these problems are working in the wrong direction for those that are too big to fail. Left alone, they will not be too effective even if they were to survive. It is extremely disappointing that companies or the society do not pay enough attention to these issues that are extremely critical for the growth and advancement of our society.

Chapter 5

Early Indicators If Any

From a point where the middle class is thriving, businesses are competing to provide better products and services, and the playing field is somewhat balanced for both the rich and the poor to a point where none of these exist is a most dramatic journey. This is what is happening in the American economy. One of our major problems as a society is not to do much or anything until the situation in question becomes a major problem. The conversion from a market economy to a finance economy did not happen overnight. It took about four decades. I lived and studied during that whole time. At least partially, this chapter is my personal account.

Every event, every change in a dynamic society presents an indicator before it happens. All indicators point out to the development of some social phenomenon. Certainly before the market economy became a finance economy there were numerous indicators, and many of them would have been considered a red flag indicating a prospective danger. Just how quickly these indicators are identified and connected to some social phenomenon is the critical aspect of using indicators. Some of them are likely to be identified way after the events have taken place, which is too late. If the indicator was a negative one, there would have been no counteractive action that was taken on time. The details presented in exhibit 5.1 are such that some of the indicators suggested some forthcoming economic

- Deregulation
- Ignoring antitrust laws
- Emphasis on budgets (budgetitis)
- Free trade (unfair)
- Dependence on foreign oil
- Losing perspectives for both political parties
- Outsourcing of major jobs
- Closing down American factories
- Considering billionaires as job creators
- Tremendous tax loopholes
- Not producing enough but bidding more for the existing
- Allowing more money into politics

Exhibit 5.1   Some of the key indicators of a move to a finance economy.

storm but, at the time, they were not correctly identified and hence there were no counteracting decisions. Let us discuss each item in exhibit 5.1.

The Shocking Recent History

Perhaps it all started with tax cuts. John F. Kennedy reduced the existing tax rates in order to counteract a recession. Just about from that point on one of the two political parties utilized tax reductions as a strategic tool. This orientation slowly eliminated the progressive nature of income tax and in time gave a tremendous economic benefit to the richest in our society. I consider tax cuts as one of the most significant movements toward the emergence of the finance economy. Tax cuts at the lower income levels could be good temporarily to fight off a recession, but if they are indicating a situation where the ultrarich are becoming richer at the expense of the society then they must be stopped. There is nothing wrong with becoming ultrarich by strong managerial and innovative powers, but in recent decades tax cuts simply created an ultrarich group in our society, which is using almost unlimited financial resources to maintain the finance economy.

Deregulation played a very important role in the emergence of the finance-driven economy. Instead of modifying and revising existing regulations, many regulations were eliminated across the board. The end result has been an economy that is running on the law of the jungle where the greedy ultrarich, who have much financial power, are eliminating competition and economic functioning as they please.

The deregulation activity, perhaps above all else, impacted the traditional market economy principle of "any attempt to reduce competition or creating monopoly power is illegal." This principle has been and is being violated by the ever-growing merger mania. As large financially well-endowed companies buy out the competitor they are creating monopoly power and weakening the existing competitive conditions in the economy. The financial power group has gained much more power by undertaking and/or by sponsoring more propaganda about the fact that if the government does not interfere the economy will work beautifully. This of course is a dangerous proposition, which supported lawlessness. Thus, the major aspects of the antitrust laws have been totally violated by ever-growing merger mania.

During the early 1980s a major emphasis regarding budgets emerged; at the time I called this the "budgetitis disease." All budgets, local, regional, national, and individual, are encouraged to be balanced. In order to accomplish this balance, cost-cutting activities rather than creating more revenues by proactive business plans were emphasized. Instead of generating more activity in revenue development additional tax cuts affected education, Medicare, social security, and research and development (R&D) budgets negatively. This was an additional effort by the 1 percenters to keep the government out of the economy and not allow some out of the ordinary events to take place.

Free trade as a major practice came about the same time. Reducing or eliminating the barriers to foreign imports made many of them extremely attractive. Many financial giants closed down domestic factories and outsourced basic essential products and particularly well-paying jobs. As American factories closed down many American well-paying middle-class jobs went to countries such as China, India, Mexico, and the like. Perhaps one of the most important aspects of free trade is its fairness. While trade took place, American producers became less and less competitive since they were accommodating the domestic pressures for avoiding pollution, facilitating requirements for fair pay for employees, and medical care as well as retirement plans. As free trade activity accelerated American factories started going abroad. As companies abandoned their US factories and built the most up-to-date factories in other countries, the remaining US plants were not taken care of properly. As a result American competitiveness further declined while the financial sector, engaged in outsourcing and joint venturing, made tremendous profits. Thus the unfair free trade worked in favor of the financial sector.

Ever since the early 1970s, the United States started becoming more and more dependent on foreign oil. First President Nixon and subsequently all of the following presidents of the country talked about "energy independence." President Carter started some efforts to create artificially generated fuel plants, which were closed down by President Reagan. Petroleum companies are partly owned by the American financial sector and this powerful sector did not want its very lucrative petroleum business to be reduced by domestic competition.

The American two-party political system worked when the parties were not too far apart and they worked together to resolve domestic and international problems of the country. But one of the two parties became much richer with the participation of its billionaire members and the two-party system became almost a football match. Each party's success became more important than solving national problems. Both of the parties forgot about the nation's needs and about initiating activities to eliminate them. Instead, each tried to nullify the other party's efforts. Thus the political system became almost totally dysfunctional. More money entered into the political system and the finance groups maintained the upper hand. Particularly the venture capital firms tried to break-even quickly and to become profitable sooner. As a result they started outsourcing as many functions as they could as early as possible. This process did not stay only with venture firms; it expanded to practically all aspects of the American economy. Thus, globalization got supercharged (Friedman 2005). Unfortunately the outsourcing of jobs that has been going on has been simply destroying the American middle class. That group has been shrinking just about since the finance economy emerged. It must be reiterated that the American superiority as a thriving, progressive, and successful country has been mainly due to its middle class. That group maintained the country's stability and hardworking nature. While many third-world countries are striving to develop a stable, steady, and progressive middle class, the current finance economy is ignoring the shrinkage of the American middle class. Again, this is a very dangerous situation and cannot be corrected unless the American society goes back to supporting and benefitting from the middle class.

The Outrageous Income Distribution

One of the most common claims that have been heard very often during the past two decades is that millionaires and billionaires are the job creators and they must be given major tax breaks. First, it has been stated in different parts of this book that start-up activity, which happened by entrepreneurial new enterprises, is primarily responsible for job creation. Second, the proposed tax cuts have done nothing more than widening the gap between the rich and the poor in our society. This point must be explored more carefully. While the country is still in a recession, the CEO pays went up again, in 2011. The average level of CEO pay in the Standard and Poor's 500 stock indexes increased 13.9 percent following a 22.8 percent increase in CEO pay in 2010. It must be reiterated that the national GDP grew very nominally during that period.

Perhaps even more shocking is that while the CEO pay was about 25–30 times greater than the wages of a typical worker (Reich 2007) it became about 380 times in 2011, which was an increase from 2010 when the ratio was 343 (AFL-CIO 2012). Even though

CEOs claim they deserve all the money increase because of the shareholder values, these values did not go up during that period. This double-digit increase in average CEO pay is an indication of what is happening in the finance economy. The top 1 percent in the income distribution is becoming more and more disconnected from the remaining 99 percent of the society (Bureau of Labor Statistics 2012). In fact, both workers and shareholders have suffered throughout the past decade. On December 31, 2010, the S&P 500 index closed 19 points below its high on March 24, 2000. The US median household income also fell by $3,719 between the years 2000 and 2010 (US Census Bureau 2012). This unrealistic CEO pay increases is one of the key factors causing income inequality in the United States. A congressional Budget Office report found that income inequality has risen dramatically with the top 1 percent receiving most of the income growth in the country between 1979 and 2007 (Congressional Budget Office 2012). Furthermore, a study indicated that in 2010, during the first year of the economic recovery from the Great Recession, the top 1 percent of the American society captured 93 percent of the growth in income (Saez 2012). Simultaneously, companies such as Wal-Mart forced its suppliers to squeeze wages and benefits of millions of workers who worked for them (Reich 2007). During these totally shocking developments in economic terms CEOs have become less like top bureaucrats and more like Hollywood celebrities or star athletes with their totally incomprehensible pay scales. Perhaps even worse is that their totally unrealistic pay raises did not have much to do with the profitability of their particular companies. In one of my earlier books I stated that the increased company profitability and CEO pay increases showed a very low correlation coefficient (Samli 2001). This reiterated the point that the CEO performance has almost nothing to do with the profitability of the company the outlandish salaries and raises do not have a logical and justifiable foundation.

In addition to manipulating extraordinary salaries and raises the financially powerful group is receiving some unbelievable tax loopholes. All petroleum companies, pharmaceutical firms, and many others have been receiving some substantial tax breaks that are strengthening the finance economy at the cost of the market economy. BP, the company that caused the most critical petroleum spill that created tremendous hardship for millions of Americans, still receives tax subsidies by the billions. It was the company's unpreparedness that caused the tremendous petroleum flow into the American beaches, which is not quite fairly paid for. Somehow the financial power group manages to influence the American government for unrealistic and not necessarily deserved economic favors.

As American factories closed down and outsourcing became rampant what was being produced in this country became more and more limited. In the meantime, the 1 percenters kept on receiving exorbitant financial revenues. This caused a tremendous explosion in the stock market. People kept on bidding more and more for the existing and not increasing production. It must be maintained here that despite the propaganda about their being job creators, millionaires and billionaires strictly played the stock market, which has no positive impact for the 99 percenters.

Perhaps the most harmful development in the American economy during the past four decades or so is the fact that much money was allowed to enter the political scene. This gave totally new and unprecedented power to the 1 percenters and clearly counteracted the democratic principle of "all men created equal." Unless this pattern is reversed, the American society is facing a very dangerous pattern of the 99 percent of the society's population being controlled and manipulated by the 1 percent.

The Dangerous Journey

This book is about the most dangerous journey our society has undertaken. Exhibit 5.2 illustrates this shocking pattern. Although it is self-explanatory and partially explained throughout this chapter, a brief description of the exhibit is presented here.

In the market economy competition and laws prevented companies from becoming dangerously big. In the finance economy, relatively less competition and not having strongly enforced laws have

	Features of a Market Economy	Features of a Finance Economy
Enterprises	Numerous small to medium	Relatively fewer and many are too big
Business decision conditions	To increase sales and reach out to most consumers	To increase profits by cost reduction catering to select customers
Information	To determine consumer needs	To determine how to exploit consumers for more pay
Consumers	Have significant multiple choices	Limited choice in oligopolistic conditions
Market entry	Very easy, not many hindrances	In many cases very difficult; must cope with oligopolistic powers
Technology	To benefit everyone	To replace workers
Pricing practices	Competitive pricing; all are price takers	Much less competitive pricing; many are price makers
Promotion	Primarily informative to help consumers	Primarily propaganda type complicating consumer attitude
Income distribution	Presence of strong middle class; relatively smaller poor population	Shrinking middle class, much of the income is in the top 1 percent group; very large group of people below poverty line

Exhibit 5.2   Continuing dangerous journey.

created a few industrial and financial giants who are taking over the entire country.

Business decisions, in an earlier market economy era, were made to increase sales to reach out to consumers and enhance the quality of life as they also made a profit. This is simply reversed in the finance economy. Businesses put more emphasis on cost reduction by trying to reduce tax rates and fees. Also they emphasize outsourcing good jobs to low-cost countries and squeezing their American workers for lower pay.

Information in this continuing dangerous journey has begun determining consumer needs and catering to them as to how to exploit consumers for better profit. This is done by using oligopoly power and limiting their choice for purchase options.

In the earlier pattern consumers received the benefits of somewhat effective competition. This meant greater choice and more reasonable prices. With the finance economy model these benefits are gone and consumers, in general, are made more uncomfortable. In the new model consumers are finding it more and more difficult to make ends meet.

Market entry was easier earlier. As the conditions changed, smaller competitive enterprises are finding it more and more difficult to enter the economy and function easily. The industrial and financial giants are blocking the entrance of lean and mean competing small firms.

In the market economy for many years technology-related productivity created a one-hour reduction in the work week. This basically meant increase in productivity benefitted everyone. Technological advancements were shared with the society as a whole. However, around the early 1980s this pattern changes. Instead of befitting the whole society, increased productivity became a tool to replace workers. The number of workers went down and profitability for a few privileged went up. The society no longer benefited by increased productivity due to technological advances.

Competitive pricing was one of the most important features of the market economy. It gave consumers a real choice to organize their finances. However, with the oligopolistic tendencies of the finance economy, price is not quite a strategic competitive tool. Oligopolists stay away from price competition. Instead, they emphasize nonprice competition, which may be product design, advertising effectiveness, reputation, and the like. Thus, consumers, who are trying to make ends meet, lose.

It is already mentioned that in the market economy promotional activities were in the direction of informing consumers. Better-informed consumers, by definition, make better choices; this would improve competition and the society as a whole would be improved. However, once again as the society moved in the direction of the finance economy promotional activities became more of a power play. The industrial and financial giants used promotion mainly to strengthen their positions rather than truly informing the populace.

The most shocking fact about the emerging finance economy is the income distribution that is taking place.

As seen in exhibit 5.3 the upper fifth of the American society received over 50 percent of the total GDP. The top 5 percent of the society received 21.3 percent while the bottom fifth of the society obtained 3.3 percent of the total income. According to estimates in 2010 the top 1 percent received 93 percent of the increase from 2009 to 2010. This questionable income distribution reveals a more dramatic story when comparisons are made between 1990 and 2010. Exhibit 5.4 illustrates a dramatic scenario. While the poorest of the income categories lost 13.2 percent the top 5 percent gained 15.1 percent. In fact more than half of the society, 80 percent to be exact, faced a net income reduction. This further indicates that the society

	0/0 of Total GDP
Lowest 20 percent	3.3
Next 20 percent	8.5
Middle 20 percent	14.6
Upper middle 20 percent	23.4
Upper 20 percent	50.2
Top 5 percent	21.3

Exhibit 5.3   Estimated income distribution in 2010.
Source: US Census Bureau of Current Population Survey.

Lowest 20 percent	−13.2
Next 20 percent	−11.5
Middle 20 percent	−8.2
Upper Middle 20 percent	−2.5
Upper 20 percent	+7.7
Top 5 percent	+15.1

Exhibit 5.4   Percentage income changes between 1990 and 2010.
Source: US Census Bureau Current Population Survey.

is in a very dangerous pattern of creating big gaps between the rich and the poor.

Not only is the top 1 percent of the population primarily calling the shots as to where the society is headed, but in recent years, this group has been given more power to use as much money as they want to influence the national political elections. The group is pressing strongly to have further income tax reductions and no laws to control their activities. This is a formula to almost destroy the American society.

Summary

Every event in a society presents early indicators. The society's task is to recognize these indicators and either support them or counteract them. During the past four decades or so, many major developments have taken place, all of which are supporting the movement from a market economy to a finance economy. But all of these events had early indicators that were totally ignored.

In this chapter 13 key indicators are listed and discussed. This is not an exhaustive list but it indicates how dangerous the current American journey is. To illustrate the developments more systematically, a comparative analysis is presented indicating the general orientation that existed in the market economy and what is happening in the current finance economy. The contrast in the practices of the market economy and the finance economy is so radical that one would easily question where is the leadership to stop what is happening to our society.

The indicators in the dramatically altered American economy with regressive tax policies, weakening labor, and deteriorating health and retirement benefits have shown themselves in the income distribution. Not only are 1 and 5 percenters receiving more than 50 percent of the total income but only the top 20 percent of the society has received an increase in their income. The rest of the society has become poorer. This is a dangerous and unsustainable situation.

Appendix: Even the Economy Is Antipoor

There is much in the earlier literature dealing with the poor paying more (Caplowitz 1963; Bagdikian 1964; Samli 1969). When the 1 percenters are in charge and the poor are charged more for essentials, the discrepancy between the rich and the poor becomes intolerable. I tried to analyze that statement by using one of my personal approaches. Instead of having a general consumer price index for the whole economy, I developed a consumer price index for the rich in our society and for the poor. I very generously identified the rich as those who have an income of $70,000 and above, and the poor having an income between $5,000 and 10,000. There are no statistics for those with an income of less than $5,000. Consumer price index is the measurement of the change in the cost of the average market basket. Since the poor and the rich do have differences in their market baskets it is not very difficult to construct a separate price index for each one of the two groups.

The unadjusted consumer price index for all urban consumers in August 2009 was 215.8 (US Bureau of Labor Statistics 2009a, b) with the base year being 1982–1984. The question here was how the poor did and the rich faired during that period. By using the consumption patterns of the rich and the poor reported in the Bureau of Labor Statistics in 2008 it was found that the cost of the market basket for the poor, which is their total consumption as consumers, has increased faster than the total cost of the whole market basket for the rich by 10.5 points. In order to develop a price index for the poor and another for the rich I utilized their respective market baskets of these two income groups. The market baskets examined in this study are composed of 14 different consumption categories, which display 100 percent of each group's consumption. In order to construct the two different price indexes each consumption category was evaluated by its own specific price index. The key differences between the two groups are presented in their consumption patterns. By using individual price index data for each consumption category in 2009 with 2008 consumer expenditure survey proportions two separate price indexes were

Using Aug 2009 CPIs with 2008 Expenditure shares[a]	$5,000–9,999 Expenditure Shares	Price Index	Columns 1 X2	$70,000 and More Expenditure Shares	Price Index	Columns 4 X5
Food at home	0.113	213.7	24.1	0.063	213.7	13.5
Food away from home	0.053	223.7	11.9	0.055	223.7	12.3
Alcoholic beverages	0.009	221.0	2.0	0.009	221	2.0
Housing	0.399	217.8	86.9	0.32	217.8	69.7
Apparel and services	0.044	117.1	5.2	0.035	117.1	4.1
Transportation	0.153	184.4	28.2	0.165	184.4	30.4
Health care	0.063	376.5	23.7	0.049	376.5	18.4
Entertainment	0.048	114.7	5.5	0.058	114.7	6.7
Personal care products and services	0.013	204.4	2.7	0.012	204.4	2.5
Reading[b]	0.002	215.8	0.4	0.002	215.8	0.4
Education	0.044	193.2	8.5	0.026	193.2	5.0
Tobacco products and smoking supplies	0.013	763.6	9.9	0.004	763.6	3.1
Miscellaneous	0.01	345.1	3.5	0.017	345.1	5.9
Personal insurance and pensions[b]	0.016	215.8	3.5	0.146	215.8	31.5
Total	1		215.9	1		205.4

Exhibit 5A.1 CPI for the rich and poor in 2009.

Source: Calculated from a Bureau of Labor Statistics Consumer Expenditure survey 2008 and price indexes from August 2009, with the base years of 1982–1984 being 100 percent, available at http://www.bls.gov/cpi/cpid0908.pdf and http://www.bls.gov/cex/2008/share/income.pdf.

Note: Calculations are based on consumer units of one person by income before taxes.

[a] Price index of individual product or service categories are weighted on the basis of the market baskets of the two income categories. The rich are defined here as those who have an annual income of more than $70,000, and the poor as those who have an income between $5,000 and $9,999.

[b] The unadjusted CPI for all urban consumers in August 2009 was used for Reading and Personal Insurance and Pensions because no specific CPI was available for those categories.

constructed in exhibit 5A.1. It can be seen that the calculated price index for the rich is 10.5 points lower than the poor consumers' price index. In other words, the cost of living has gone up faster for the poor than for the rich, thereby creating a hidden discrimination against the poorest sector of our economy. That difference translates to 5 percent of the total GDP. If that 5 percent of GDP is calculated on the basis of total 2009 GDP, then it becomes about $715 billion dollars (US Bureau of Economic Analysis 2009). Exhibit 5A.1 shows that the poor are paying for certain consumption categories in different proportions than the rich. This is making their cost of living higher than that of the rich. The poor in general are using more of their overall income than the rich on food at home, housing, health care, education, and tobacco products. Even though they are not paying more for those items than their wealthy counterparts, the pattern is creating more of a problem for the poor. These categories multiplied with their respective price indexes are giving the poor a significantly higher total cost of living than the rich. Thus it becomes clear that the poor are facing greater hardship than the rich. In short, *the poor pay more*.

Perhaps the shocking fact of this alarming analysis is that I have used the same technique to find out that since as early as the late 1960s the same pattern has been prevailing. In other words the poor have been paying more. Thus they are not only poor but also the economy is against their well-being. If these calculations were replicated only for the 1 percenters the discrepancy between the rich and 99 percenters may be even greater. As can be seen, even the economy is antipoor. And therefore the rich are winning, in this case without even trying. Much needs to be done to level the playing field. A solid market economy with certain enforced regulation is a necessity for the future of our society. Early studies of this type should have been indicators of where our economy is headed and by now there should have been corrective measures. However, I believe the conditions are getting worse for the fast-growing poor section of our society.

Chapter 6

The Innovation Culture: Where Are You?

A major innovation that I call a radical innovation is likely to create major increases in employment, to provide a platform for new industries to emerge, to generate major revenues, and overall enhance the existing quality of life further (Samli 2011).

It is through innovation that countries could develop new products that are globally attractive. The sales of these would generate major revenues and help economies grow. It is through innovations that there will be a wave of entrepreneurial start-up companies emerging. They will create many new jobs. Similarly, a wave of new industries will emerge. They will also contribute to economic development (de Brittani 2000; Samli 2012b).

There is almost no possibility to measure the impact of the industrial revolution, which started with the steam engine, or the impact of the electric motor, landline telephones, and more currently mobile phone technologies. All of these started new industries and generated large sums of income for nations. Thus, radical innovations that are costly and risky can bring large economic benefits to all. Radical innovations are most likely to be developed by smaller start-up companies. These companies create jobs and expand quickly (Friedman 2010; Samli 2011). However, as discussed in different parts of this book, financially powerful industrial giants buy these dynamic start-ups and put them out of existence (or incorporate them into a point of no identity). These financial giants prefer the status quo rather than promoting a risky and wild invention that is not even developed yet. Thus, they go for more incremental innovations of improving their existing products, which are safe and reasonably profitable in the short run, rather than risking a lot of money and time by supporting disruptive technologies that are used to generate radical innovations. The radical innovations are much more geared to generating results in the long run. As the economy becomes more finance controlled or finance directed there are fewer major innovations, if any, that are radical. But, as Kao (2007) stated: a nation that does not support its basic scientific knowledge generation and exploration is flirting with doom. At the writing of this book pessimism about America's future is growing and is partially connected to the poor showing of its innovational activity (Mandel 2008). This situation is strongly related to the American economy's changing from a market economy to a finance economy where innovational research is not encouraged. The finance economy does not believe in high-risk and high-cost explorations. It deals in very short-run and least-risky undertakings. This situation is likely to get worse; the American economy is no longer number one in the world as the innovating country. Of course, this lack of progress in innovations will take the United States out of the point of being the major industrial power in the world and will put the country along with third-world countries where innovations are not common place (Mandel 2009).

Not only during a recessionary era, but in a continuing manner an ambitious country must be cultivating its innovational path for future growth and development. If the country can generate some major innovations the finance group as well as the whole country will benefit, but this point is not well understood. Currently, American innovativeness is struggling. Perhaps the most important point here is that at the present time a culture of innovation is not present and in a finance economy it may never become a reality again. It is important, however, to analyze just how the American innovation culture can be revitalized and brought back to function as it was for many decades. This chapter attempts to explore the fundamental background of an innovation culture.

The Key: Triple Helix

The presence of a well-functioning innovation culture requires an aura of positive productivity. This particular aura exists only when the triple helix of innovation is functioning (Etzkowitz et al. 2005). Exhibit 6.1 illustrates the triple helix. It is composed of government, education, and business. If the three components of the helix are not functioning positively in a coordinated manner, the society does not have a culture of innovation. The presence of a culture of innovation means basically that there is a positive atmosphere among the government, the institutions of higher learning, and the business sector. They are all in the same mode of developing an environment that is very conducive to progressive innovativeness. At this point in time, this is almost simply a dream.

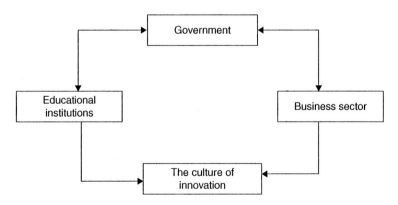

Exhibit 6.1 The triple helix.

Progressive Innovativeness

Above all, in a country there must be stimuli for innovation and a capacity to innovate (Prajojo and Ahmed 2006). Just where does innovation begin and how is it cultivated? Perhaps the most critical point here is that it is not how a lot of money or resources are available but how much knowledge is being generated and utilized (Kao 2007; Samli 2012b). In other words, without a certain level of knowledge base nothing is likely to happen. It can be maintained that even through the pieces of innovation are in place in the United States this delicate process is not properly nurtured by the finance economy. Here the key is the lack of commitment to innovation. Such a commitment means that there is a strong intention to develop and continue a stable and long-term geared innovational activity (Morgan and Hunt 1994; Samli and Weber 2000). Again this intention is totally missing in the current finance economy.

Exhibit 6.2 presents nine critical forces that would generate and maintain a powerful innovation activity. Any country, any government is obligated to cultivate these forces for the future of a country.

The whole process is totally dependent on a knowledge foundation without which there will not be an innovation culture (Kao 2007; Samli 2012b). Unless there is a certain level of educational threshold, nothing will happen. Currently, the American educational system is not adequately providing the necessary stimuli to learn more, to explore, and subsequently to innovate. The education funds are shrinking and research funds are drying up. Innovations and individual independence on creative pursuits are compromised in favor of short-run profit motives (Samli 2012b). Thus, curiosity cultivation is not present.

With excessive profit orientation in the short run, thinking and planning for the future are deemphasized. The future that is presented by the finance economy is very dubious. Currently, the preoccupation with the present and benefits for 1 percenters are so strong

Necessary Conditions	Implications
Knowledge base development	There are enough educated people to innovate
Curiosity cultivation	Serious challenges for curiosity to explore
Identifying the desired future	Having mature and ambitious goals
Keeping a constant state of evolution	Understanding the dynamic nature of the economy
Emphasizing radicalism	Cultivating radical innovation efforts
Generating the necessary talent	Making sure there is proper motivation and education
Creating a futuristic orientation	Not concentrating on present conditions, looking for improvements
Balancing applied versus basic research	Researching current problems as well as future explorations
Putting special emphasis on radical innovations	Understanding the major innovational progress that will come from radicalism

Exhibit 6.2   Progressive innovativeness.
Source: Adapted and revised from Samli (2012b).

that there is hardly any thought of what might happen in a matter of one or two decades in the future.

If the future directions are not clearly identified it is not even logical to think about the constant state of evolution. It is known that major innovative breakthroughs, which are results of constant states of evolution, would yield great benefits but they take much time and resources. Good short-run results and quick payoffs, which are generally preferred by the financial giants, are not facilitating major innovational progress. In fact, as Christensen (2003) stated, most larger companies, or bailouts as Friedman (2010) calls them, become vulnerable to radical innovations in the longer run and therefore overemphasize the short run. Thus, radical innovations that are desperately needed are not encouraged (Samli 2012b). Hence, the current recession is lingering on.

Without putting enough emphasis on people and hence not generating entrepreneurial capital an innovation culture cannot be developed. Unfortunately, that is the state of the current American experience. There simply must be individuals who are willing to take the risk of starting up new businesses, promoting innovations, and developing new activities. Creation of such an innovative milieu is totally essential, but such a milieu must be planned, developed, and maintained. Unfortunately, such an orientation, at this point in time, is not even an issue that is being discussed or pursued.

The finance economy is much more interested in short-run reasonable results and hence emphasizes short-run applied research that would yield more financial gains for a select few. That group does not appear to be very much interested in the desperately needed innovational radicalism.

Just what needs to be done and how could that be achieved? These questions take us back to the triple helix. Just what are the responsibilities of the three most important elements of innovational progress? These elements of innovational progress or the triple helix are discussed here in some detail.

Government

As seen in exhibit 6.1, government is the first prong of the triple helix. The US government has been very successful in the past in initiating and providing support for major innovational activities. The US government not only encouraged but partially financed research and development activity for a long time. This support benefited start-up entrepreneurs in many undertakings. The US government played an important role in practically all major innovational activities from space exploration to the emergence of the Internet. While under financial and political pressures this role is dwindling, the Chinese and Singaporean governments are making significant progress in supporting innovational activities in their countries. It must be specified that global competition is constantly increasing consumer information, global ethics, greening, and production efficiency among other forces and making it more important and challenging to be involved in innovation. While global stakes are extremely high the finance economy is specifying that government should not have a major role in such activities and should not spend money. Major US organizations such as the National Institute of Health or National Science Foundation are facing major budget cuts. This is because the finance economy is trying to maintain the share of the 1 percenters of GDP. Blocking futuristic innovations financially is a surefire way to make the United States a struggling third-world country.

It is essential that there must be a national proinnovation strategy, which presently does not exist. The elements of such a strategy are presented in exhibit 6.3.

As Porter (2008, p. 39) stated very bluntly: "The stark truth is that the U.S. has no long-term economic strategy, no coherent set of policies to ensure competitiveness over the long haul." Just what would be included in such a strategy is shown in exhibit 6.3. The exhibit is not exhaustive but points out some of the most important

Factors	Implications
Investment research	Making sure that among some failures there will be outstanding winners
Improving public schools	The educational foundation of a national innovation strategy begins here
Social progress must include businesses	As a very important group businesses must be encouraged to innovate
Emphasizing changing competition	The changing practices should not hold progress back
Powerful research projects must be supported	Ability to understand certain daring research activities
Developing new structures	Certain organizations must be encouraged to govern innovation-supporting programs

Exhibit 6.3   Elements of a proinnovation national strategy.
Source: Adapted and revised from Porter (2008).

elements that would generate and maintain an innovation culture development strategy that is totally missing.

The first point in the exhibit implies that if there is a basic interest in innovation it begins with research. What kind of research? How much research? What are the expected outcomes? Are all very critical questions that need to be carefully explored? But one point is very clear—without a solid educational foundation there cannot be good research.

Improving and supporting public schools is a major foundation for any kind of economic progress. Bok (2006) has asserted that our youth are running short on critical areas such as writing, critical thinking, quantitative skills, and moral reasoning. In short, with the major budget cuts and other financial pressures our education system is not delivering what it should for innovation.

If there is an innovational strategy, it simply has to have full cooperation of the business sector. Such a strategy would not materialize if the business sector does not know or does not want to cooperate. The latter is the description of the business sector behavior in the finance economy. The question here is how to get the business sector to participate in more risky and long-run innovation projects that would benefit the whole society and not simply 1 percenters in the short run.

A national innovation strategy must be flexible enough to focus on competitive realities of the economy. This means not being tied down to basic policies that do not generate the needed innovation atmosphere.

Certain research projects are more promising and hence must be supported more readily. Just having the ability to identify these and put them in the national innovation strategy is absolutely a must. But, again, at this point in time the American economy is not emphasizing such an orientation.

Finally, a national strategy cannot be developed without having a structural organization such as a national foundation of proactive research. If there is a major commitment to innovation there will be a series of organizations to see to it that innovation-related activities will become a reality. It has been maintained that economies left alone do not support innovational effort well to begin with (Lundwall 2007); the negative orientation of the finance economy when added to this creates is a big hindrance. A national system is not even present to support major innovation activities that are desperately needed.

Educational Institutions

Universities not only must pursue information generation, decision-making, and problem solving for the prevailing economic condition in the present but also must emphasize entrepreneurial development efforts as currently seen in China and Singapore (Tan 2003; Zhang and Yang 2006; Samli 2009b). I believe there is a strong bond between entrepreneurial efforts and innovation cultivation. It is critical that universities go beyond standard educational activity and develop entrepreneurial thinking that would lead to proactive innovation. Universities and other institutions of higher learning must have a generally accepted plan of action for the whole country. Exhibit 6.4 presents such a general plan. By definition, at a given time there are numerous ideas for opportunities that would cultivate major innovations. It is critical that certain universities are perhaps appointed and partially supported by the government. They must be capable of identifying the innovational opportunities.

The innovational opportunities, after being evaluated and prioritized, face the next step, that is, identifying the core competencies that are needed for these projects. Here, there may be certain areas of deficiencies that need to be corrected. If they continue to exist there will be no possibility of having the planned innovational objectives becoming a reality.

Developing the scientific and theoretical innovation plans as quickly and as carefully as possible is the essence of the educational prong of the triple helix. But only a few educational institutions pursue such a goal.

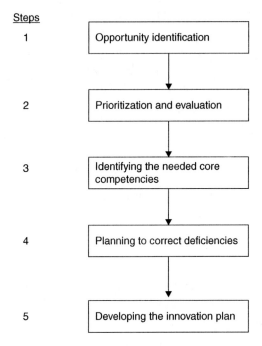

Steps

1   Opportunity identification

2   Prioritization and evaluation

3   Identifying the needed core competencies

4   Planning to correct deficiencies

5   Developing the innovation plan

Exhibit 6.4   Educational support for innovation.
Source: Adapted and revised from Samli (2009b).

It is the role of the major research universities to cultivate the three steps that are presented in exhibit 6.5, which presents a blue print for radical innovations. The active imagination, leading to creativity and generating the necessary innovations, must be the model to be adopted and used by all educational institutions.

This is a simplified version of a very complex issue that would facilitate the much needed and mainly ignored development of radical innovations (Samli 2011). It illustrates that radical innovations are a joint product of imagination and creativity. Both of these features need to be generated by the universities. In essence, major breakthroughs or radical innovations involve high levels of intelligence without which the current innovation gap cannot be eliminated (Glynn 1996). As seen in exhibit 6.5, the imagination

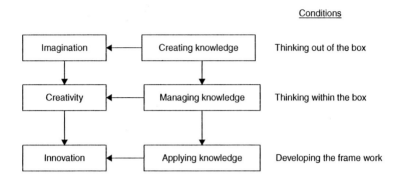

Exhibit 6.5   The three steps of radical innovations.

stage leads to creating the basic knowledge that is the essence of the whole process. But this knowledge needs to be cultivated. Here the universities will have to create close ties with the business sector. Understanding electricity was not nearly as important until the development of electric motors. This stage of innovational activity has to be a joint product of the university and private-sector prongs of the triple helix even though they do not generate quick revenues and hence are too costly. But both of these prongs are ignored or even counteracted in the finance economy because they do not yield quick revenues.

Without the contribution of the university prong the business sector emphasizes status-quo, which is the comfort zone of the finance economy. Here in order to generate a breakthrough special efforts are needed, which will stimulate imagination. Critical thinking, which is thinking out of the box, is considered to be the most important stimulator of imagination (Osborn 1953). However, this very important element of the original market economy is being put, first, out of context and, second, out of existence in the finance economy.

As indicated in exhibit 6.5 creating and managing knowledge are exercises in futility until and unless knowledge is applied (Plsek 1997). Thus, the role of the business sector in the triple helix of innovation becomes pronounced.

The Business Sector

In the market economy marketing has given consumers the products that they did not even know they needed. But when they started using these products their quality of life became substantially improved. This has been accomplished by the business sector prong of the triple helix. The corporate entities must once again apply the knowledge and manage the risk factor to generate outstanding or radical innovations. But currently, the giant corporate entities are buying each other out and laying off workers; these activities are not conducive to innovational progress (Bloomberg Business Week 2012c). Large industrial giants have been in existence long enough to reach certain economic level and comfort status. This status in the finance economy is about an equilibrium position where there is no zeal to move forward. When there is such a state of lack of ambition for further development, the society does not advance economically. In a recession period this situation becomes critically disruptive and rather dangerous.

Problems of Industrial Giants

As Christensen (2003) states, companies stumble for many reasons. Among these are: bureaucracy, arrogance, tired executive blood, poor planning, inadequate skills, and short-term orientation. In chapter 2 some of these are discussed in some detail. Currently, all of these problems are a reality and the finance economy is doing nothing about them. The old established companies are in their comfort zones and they are in charge of the economy; hence, they are more interested in buying out competition and laying off workers. They are preoccupied with cost cutting or modifying existing products rather than exploring new and somewhat risky, but totally necessary, ventures. They are not challenged by competition and are enjoying their comfort zones, which are prevalent in the finance economy. Competition is the key element of the market economy.

Exhibit 6.6 displays why and how the finance-driven giants act counter to innovation. The exhibit is self-explanatory. It displays a wrong type of orientation connected to rigidity toward change and decision-making, and also connected to short-run financial orientation. All of these conditions are creating extremely antimajor innovational explorations and progress. Very briefly, financial giants are using the existing technologies for quick and fast returns. They are controlled by very tight bureaucracies who are rigid and extremely selfish. In addition to being rigid and selfish these bureaucracies are very arrogant in controlling the functional activities of financial giants. But at the same time, these bureaucracies are extremely out of touch. They do not pay attention to progressive movements in the society. If you are paying more attention to your current well-being, by definition, the necessary skills for sustainability and societal progress are not developed and therefore skills for progress and societal development become inadequate. Finally, the short-term orientation

Counterinnovation Conditions	Implications
Using sustaining technologies	They do not want to change disruptive technologies that create innovational breakthroughs
Bureaucracy	Tied down to certain practices and do not want to change
Arrogance	They are in charge and what got them here is good enough
Out of touch	Being tied down to certain practices causing them to be out of touch in new developments
Inadequate skills	As technological progress takes place the rigid top decision making group display inadequate skills
Short-term orientation	Making quick financial gains in the short run is good enough

Exhibit 6.6 Counterinnovation conditions that exist in finance driven giants.

of the 1 percenters is not providing any hope of chance for the society to make progress for future.

When the business sector does not cooperate the whole triple helix of innovation becomes dysfunctional. For an industrial society such as the United States the presence of a dysfunctional triple helix is extremely dangerous. The lack of innovations and the resultant lack of economic progress will put the country among the third-world countries. Those countries are struggling to survive and, with some hope, to show some economic progress.

One of the most glorious achievements of the market economy era was the emergence and success of the Silicon Valley. Many entrepreneurial innovators started numerous businesses and the whole activity became a big success. In another book I suggested that there should be numerous facsimiles of the Silicon Valley so that the society would enjoy the benefits of having a few organized activities dedicated to creating innovations to enhance the general economic well-being. These facsimiles would be very beneficial particularly in the current recession that the American economy is experiencing.

These facsimiles accomplish a few unique undertakings. Among these are attracting and cultivating some of the best minds, developing intellectual atmosphere, cultivate entrepreneurial cultures, generating and supporting cutting-edge research, encouraging networking trust and commitment among teams, and many others. However, unfortunately, the current finance economy does not consider fully supporting Silicon Valley let alone creating a number of facsimiles (Samli 2009). Having a successful blue print such as the Silicon Valley and not using this model to develop numerous facsimiles is totally inexcusable; but it is happening.

Summary

It is impossible to measure the economic and psychological benefits of previous innovations such as sewing machines, the polio vaccine, and the Internet among myriads of others. But we know that these innovations have changed our lives as they also generated considerable return to the companies that developed them. This is what happened in the United States throughout the market economy that the country experienced. In this chapter we explored the deterioration of the innovational progress that has been experienced in this society primarily by the emergence of the finance economy.

In order to understand the negative impact of the finance economy the innovation process is described by the three prongs of the innovation helix: government, educational institutions, and business sector.

Under much political pressure the government at all levels has been cutting the education budgets, redirecting the research funds to military, and is not at all involved in the development or implementation of a national strategy. As a result, the all-important first prong of the triple helix of innovation, in the presence of finance economy, is not even there.

Educational institutions are left alone in an uncoordinated manner. The five-step plan for innovation support that is presented in this chapter is not functional partly because of the nonexistent national innovation support strategy and partly because there are no coordinated university efforts. Without a coordinated plan for innovational progress in general the universities become powerless to come up with a coordinated plan of their own.

It is maintained in this chapter that the third prong of the triple helix is the payoff of the whole process, which is primarily implemented by the business sector. The business sector in the finance economy is quite content with receiving fast revenues in the short run, with not moving out of their comfort zone, with being in charge even though they are not helping the economy as a whole. Thus the finance-driven business sector is not interested in investing in risky and futuristic investments that are desperately needed for the future of the American society.

Chapter 7

Recessions Are Totally Man Made

Despite the accumulated knowledge about our economy, we have not quite learned what needs to be done if and when a recession takes place. Recessions have a strong impact on the existing economic status, but their negative impacts are not articulated and not counteracting them is carefully analyzed and practiced. Recessions are very costly and disruptive; however, instead of developing rational and objective orientation toward counteracting them and indeed even stopping them before they materialize, there have been tendencies to treat them as almost natural phenomena and explaining them with political and financial doctrines. This situation does not contribute to the well-being of the poor, the elderly, and small businesses but does have certain powerful, questionable, but beneficial impact on the 1 percent rather than the remaining 99 percent as the current literature and politicians describe the very alarming current income dichotomy in our society.

In general, this author, who has observed and studied some 14 recessions in a long professional life, maintains that both public as well as the private sectors of our economy must learn to stop recessions before they cause severe economic damage to the whole society. In addition to emphasizing the need for joint effort to counteract recessions this chapter presents a model showing how recessions can be counteracted and how efforts to help resurrect the market economy once again can be successfully performed. The implications of this present chapter are extremely critical for the economic well-being of the American society as a whole and must be carefully researched and discussed.

Just What Is a Recession?

A major slowing down in the prevailing economic activity is called a "recession." A typical recession increases the number of unemployed by millions very quickly. It cuts down, if any, the progress in GDP; it causes hundreds of thousands of small businesses to fail. Each failing business has major costs incurred to the economy. Losing investments in businesses combined with individual bankruptcies cause much loss to the economy and to individuals. Furthermore, discouraged investments in the form of business expansions are additional and uncalculated losses. Additionally, in today's global economy, a recession that begins in the United States or, say, in Europe can easily spread out to many other countries that are trading partners (Krugman 1999; Stiglitz 2002). In such cases, another uncalculated but rather serious economic loss will occur. Thus, the cost and ill effects of recessions, particularly on national and international economic activities, are not properly understood and hence are not counteracted.

It is extremely disheartening that at the down of the twenty-first century even though we are advanced enough to have the military might to destroy the world, the capability to travel much faster than the speed of sound, or to eliminate one of the most devastating diseases such as polio, we have not learned how to cope with economic recessions appropriately. The cost of recession to the society as discussed here is excessive enough to warrant much more attention from the government and the business sector than current practices show. It is time to abandon the near-theological reasoning such as lack of balanced budgets or government interferences, which are creating business cycles, and develop an open mind toward counteracting the extremely ill effects of recessions. It is posited here that the business and government sectors working closely can function optimally to counteract the ill effects of sharp cynical fluctuations, which are affecting all of us, and generate favorable antirecessionary conditions.

The Power of Recessions

In every decade during the second half of the twentieth century there has been at least one recession. It must be reiterated that recessions are very costly not only for the society as a whole but for too many businesses and millions of workers individually. This situation disrupts society's economic progress and creates tremendous hardship on, particularly, those who cannot afford it.

At no time in history have we accumulated more information about our economy and failed to use that information for the advancement of the society or counteracting recessions. Eliminating recessions or easing off their devastating impact would truly contribute to the economic advancement of our society. At this writing, the American economy is experiencing its deepest and most far-reaching recession, which it has been struggling to combat. During the past four decades, our position toward recessions has changed from one of "realistic" to one of "indoctrination" perhaps partially by the financial rather than market economy perceptions. This movement created a situation closer to dogmatic orientation such as if we get government out of business and cut taxes for the billionaires the recession would disappear. This dogmatic point of view remained strong even though proven to be wrong. In the Clinton years, the taxes for the very rich went up and the government took a more proactive approach. There were over 22 million jobs created as opposed to George W. Bush's tax cuts and creation of about 6 million new jobs.

Adam Smith's simplistic model of a market economy, that is, that free and uninterrupted markets work perfectly, could have been factual in the eighteenth- and perhaps at the beginning of nineteenth-century economies. However, this stance must be rejected on the basis of our experiences in the twentieth century

(Krugman 2000). The Great Depression did not end until FDR had a powerful proactive orientation. The early 1990s recession ended when a major effort was made on emphasizing information technology and high-tech.

However, the current recession is not quite eliminated because of the fact that the political parties are not working jointly to fight it off. Political groups, instead of trying to eliminate or at least curb recessions quickly as they emerge, have been playing politics at the expense of the society.

Under normal circumstances a progressive society would make economic advancement a major goal not only for a few privileged but for all (Ryan 1981). It would provide equal educational opportunity to the citizenry and fair and progressive medical services, and would facilitate industrial growth by maintaining or even improving the infrastructure. The progressive society must make sure the competition and consumer values are properly maintained and further improved.

Unfortunately, recessions create more negative impact on the lower end of the economic spectrum. Furthermore, they are beneficial to the 1 percent group, which has much financial resources to survive the recession. As specified earlier too-big-to-failers would not risk to undertake a profitable and dangerous activity if they are not doing well. The financial giants are too big to fail in recessions, or they are socialistic, but if they are doing well in economic boom times they are very capitalistic. The savings and loan fiasco in the early 1990s caused the American society about 500 billion dollars. The housing bubble in 2008 has created a most dangerous recession and in both cases the too-big-to-failers were saved by the US government. But in the meantime widespread business failures created great opportunities for financial equity companies to go in and make billions of dollars of profits at the cost of the 99 percent of our society. In such situations reductions in or the elimination of retirement programs and having a large unemployment group to choose from and pay lower salaries have made the 1 percent much happier and much richer. This is how the 1 percent is receiving about 91 percent of the total GDP created by the mighty American economy. This situation encourages recessions but in reality this type of unequal distribution of GDP cannot be sustained. This is a dangerous situation; in the world economic history such conditions have created class warfare. Our economy, certainly, is not immune to such a development. This particular pattern that is dividing our country is further stimulated by simplistic clichés such as privatization, or deregulation, or tax cuts for the rich. Our economy has become too complex and too manipulated for the average citizen to truly understand and act accordingly. This is why the too-big-to-failers, once they receive help from the federal government, turn around and help support a small government with limited tax revenues, so that some other risky and wild undertaking by them will not be stopped by the government. This type of orientation, strongly supported by the finance economy, would have been totally blocked by the market economy.

The too-big-to-failers are trying to create a Medicare system that is at least partially privatized and will create much income for the insurance industry and almost devastate the poor or the middle class.

Similarly there are constant pressures by the financial power groups to reduce or even eliminate social security. Such financial pressures have a much stronger impact in a recession because the federal government does not have a powerful financial stance. Thus the rich survive and benefit; the poor and middle class get hurt. This is what Samli (1998; 2001) has named "survival of the fattest." Industrial giants could survive recessions because they have large resources to draw from whereas small, lean, mean competing machines fail because they have no reserves. As a result while large firms survive and even prosper the dynamic start-ups fail. The society does not make progress; in fact, it regresses because those that survive, say, the bailouts, do not create employment, do not innovate, just continue as is, and perhaps even make more money in the process.

Furthermore, the billionaires are not ambitious enough to start new businesses and suffer through the growth pains. They prefer to play the stock market and put their money in Swiss banks and in other tax-free alternatives.

Since Adam Smith's (2012) description of the economy that "invisible hands" make the adjustments in the economy there have been many claims not to interfere with the movements of the economy. However, as seen in a number of recent recessions the invisible hands appear to be on the side of the rich and punishing the poor for being poor.

The economy can and should make adjustments in critical areas such as the economic development, industrialization, income distribution, employment, and the like. However, if there are no regulations and the economy is totally left alone the law of the jungle steps in and favors the 1 percenters since they have the financial brute power. This situation damages the society and its progress.

Conventional Wisdom

Almost in all recessions, even though it is proven not to work, there is a major Federal Reserve intervention in terms of reducing interest rates with the hopeful assumption that cheaper money would stimulate attempts to expand from the supply side. The Federal Reserve in short uses monetary policy to combat recessions. However, it appears that this attempt does not work. Exhibit 7.1 illustrates four major recessions during the past three decades. The fifth is just continuing at the writing of this chapter. As can be seen, significant reductions in interest rates took place in every recession. Although it may have had some minor impact in combatting the recession it has not eliminated the recession. The conventional wisdom is that by manipulating finances from the top the recession can be stopped. Even though this orientation has been in existence for a long while, it is not effective. The key point in recessions is that there must be demand in the economy for goods and services so that there will be jobs created. In other words the key remedy for recessions is not on the supply side but on the demand side. But most of the money is accumulating in the hands of the 1 percenters, there is no job security, and large-scale unemployment is simply not conducive to starting businesses and creating new jobs. Thus, the most powerful

Recession Beginning Date	Interest Rate	Recession Ending Date	Interest Rate
October 1970	6.2	February 1972	3.29
January 1981	19.08	December 1982	8.95
January 1991	6.91	December 1992	8.95
January 2001	5.98	December 2001	1.82
October 2008	4.00	Just Beginning	–

Exhibit 7.1 Beginning and reduced interest rates during the four major recessions.

Source: http://www.federalreserve.gov/releases/h15/data.html.

tool to fight back recessions, that is, creating jobs, is not very easy. "If there is a recession we must use monetary policy and lower interest rates, because cheap money will stimulate economic activity" is not an acceptable proposition. Many analysts have concluded that with monetary policy the duration of the recession cannot be cut short (Diebold and Rudebusch 2001). Not only does cheap money not provide an adequate stimulus to create jobs but also it would not go deep into the recession and reverse it. Perhaps it is critical to point out that this situation has been described as the "liquidity trap" as early as mid-1930s, which means that cheap money is not attractive enough since there are no market opportunities (Keynes 1936); the United States and Japan have come close to experiencing such a liquidity trap (Krugman 2000). Thus, what truly would jump-start the economy during a recession is not quite understood since the proponents of monetary policy created much, in reality ineffective, discussion on the value of monetary theory. It is very conceivable that even though it did not do much to combat recession, monetary policy was very attractive to the 1 percenters to pay off their debts by using cheap money (Samli 1998; 2001).

Enter Fiscal Policy

Many have advocated that fiscal policy is a necessity to jump-start the economy during a recession. Here it is critical to understand the role of fiscal policy. In all recessions there is a high level of unemployment, which indicates that the industrial sector is not functioning at its full capacity and there is no benefit of economies of scale. Unused industrial capacity is a sure indication of higher costs of production than what would be if the full capacities are used and economies of scale will provide lower costs. In a recession the critical goal is to increase the use of the unused productive capacity. This means utilizing the unemployed to produce cheaper products by using excess capacity in the industrial sector created by the recession. The important issue here is to generate an immediate increase in the aggregate demand so that employment is created and the utilization of the unused productive capacity is increased. Just how this can be accomplished has been an important debate topic numerous times without a satisfactory conclusion. However, the following rationale needs to be carefully considered. In generating immediate aggregate demand it is important also to generate consumption income that will immediately penetrate into the market. In other words those who are likely to spend whatever they have, that is, the poor, must be given more money immediately. Here, the existing money must go to those who would spend the money immediately, which means selective tax cuts along with job creation. Germany during the recent recession has split existing jobs to give more money to the unemployed. In such situations, there is no way of thinking of deficit cutting by reducing government spending. Perhaps one additional point here is to help those individuals who have been outsourcing to in-source by helping them financially. In other words, the fiscal policy must be implemented at different levels very selectively to counteract the recession. It must be reiterated that tax breaks for the middle class and working poor are more functional than tax breaks for the rich, because the lower-income people will use the money immediately for their necessities.

Propensity to Consume

Propensity to consume is the relationship between income and consumption. It is also referred to as *consumption function*. The concept does not mean only a desire to consume but the actual consumption that takes place or is likely to take place. As income grows the immediacy of consumption, that is, propensity to consume, decreases. This simply means that giving tax cuts to millionaires in a recession is not likely to work immediately. Propensity to consume goes down because of the lack of urgency or immediacy of the need for consumption on the part of the rich. Thus, the faster the tax breaks reach the lower-income groups, the faster is the immediate possibility of creating jobs. But there is also a very important provision—if consumers feel that their jobs are in jeopardy they will not spend. Thus, a job security program, even with lower pay, must be present for the fiscal policy solutions to work.

Once again, while monetary policy trying to manage the recession from the top does not work, managing it by using fiscal policy that is trying to combat it from the bottom is likely to work. In other words, the market economy orientation from the bottom is likely to work whereas the finance economy orientation from the top does not work. As opposed to reducing capital gains tax, which is proposed in every recession, an investment tax credit, which would directly encourage enterprises to replace the old technology with the modern, not only would create jobs immediately, but will also provide progress in the future. Again, instead of tax cuts for the billionaires, if there were to be a tax incentive to hire new workers, or at least not to fire current employees it would make a significant counter-recessionary impact. Additionally, not providing tax breaks for the outsourcers for exporting American jobs, but giving tax advantages for those who are insourcing, bringing those jobs that went overseas back to the United States, would not only work immediately but also make a positive impact on the country's economic growth in the future. These are some of the major fiscal policy alternatives that are likely to counteract recessions. This author, in the middle of the current "great recession," has seen American workers who are going to lose their jobs training the Chinese workers to take over, which, again, is going to benefit the finance group as it damages the American economy.

One of the most important aspects of a counter-recessionary strategy is spending, which is buying products and services that mean more consumption by the lower-economic groups. This certainly does not happen all by itself. If the 99 percenters were to split jobs, just as discussed earlier, which is being done in Germany, rather that laying off workers, combined with lowering prices and increasing credit availability would have significant impact, which can be implemented only by the start-ups and not by the bailouts. Bailout in recessions stop spending, lay off workers, and outsource jobs out of the country. The distinction between the approach of the 1 percenters versus the 99 percenters to recession clearly indicates that moving from a market economy to a finance economy does not pay for the country's economy. As the 1 percenters insist taking government out of the picture clearly will make the situation much worse. Despite all the claims to the contrary, businesses, even the financial giants, would not spend if the government is not spending; the much forgotten argument that in recessions government must spend and not cut down spending must be reiterated. President Eisenhower started the interstate highway system as spending to battle recession. President Clinton stopped the 1991 recession by increasing spending on high-tech and information technologies. However, at the writing of this book, President Obama is not able to start a much need infrastructure improvement activity because the most powerful 1 percenters are blocking it (Diebold and Rudebusch 2001). In fact, the dogmatic point of view that "government should not spend, the consumers should" is a display of lack of understanding, the "spending domino effect." However, it must be reiterated that government alone cannot possibly counteract recessions. The situation desperately needs cooperation from the business sector.

The Role of Business

Any business, big or small, must ask the question, "shall I combat recession now or wait." If the answer is "now" then the next question becomes "how?" It is unfortunately clear that there has not been enough research on this very critical area, and most businesses do not even know what the available alternatives are. But one thing must be made very clear—without positive participation by all to combat recession nothing would be enough to overcome it. As mentioned earlier, the financial giants can wait and may even benefit from the recession whereas the lean, mean, competing machines of the 99 percenters cannot survive. The society as a whole must go beyond the political propaganda and fight off recession before it blooms fully. In such cases the whole society experiences the economic ill effects, which must be avoided. After about 14 recessions, this author believes that there should be some basic general rules that the society should follow at the first indication of a forthcoming recession. The rule must be the market economy orientation from the bottom-up rather than finance economy orientation from the top-down. The differences between the two options are almost like that of night and day.

Conventional Wisdom Once Again

In their reactive modes, many businesses in recessionary times do at least two wrong things. First they lay off workers, and second, they cut down expenditures. This particular two-pronged route refuels the recessionary pressures rather than combatting them. Typically by laying off people firms not only help shrink total market demand but also lose part of the human resource capabilities of the society. In such cases human resources do not contribute to the well-being of the society but also of those who lose their jobs who happened to be specialists in their activities, no longer work and hence there appears a weakened core competency of the society's human resource performance. Similarly, by cutting down their expenditures firms may be minimizing their promotional activity and services among others and as a result not helping the necessary demand for goods and services to take place. This situation may further cause an accelerated decline in the total sales volume of the society. Such cases, by definition, create or accelerate the negative impact of recessions.

The 2001 recession lasted a long time because of the additional cost-cutting factors. Cost cutting in a recession is a contributor to the economic slowdown. Also, during that time many American companies have been engaged in outsourcing of many high-paying jobs in the United States for much lower salaries in India or China. Thus the US economy was very slow in creating enough new jobs to combat recession. Additionally, increased productivity has created more temptation on the part of the financial giants to lay off even more people rather than creating new jobs. After all, if much growth is not expected to take place in the prevailing economy, cost cutting becomes more attractive for the bailouts. Start-ups by definition must create jobs and spend. Thus while the bailouts very selfishly try to maintain their lucrative economic level by cutting cost and laying off people, the start-ups do just the opposite. Obviously, it is not the first group but the second that is combatting the recession. At the same time, lesser consumer demand for goods and services in the United States caused by the recession generated lower profits or losses leading to shutting down of finished goods plants in the United States (Dillard 1948). Thus, the key consideration of absorbing the unemployed at the end of the recession did not take place quickly and the 2001 recession continued for over three years (Orphanides 2004). The lack of expansionistic tendencies on the part of the industrial giants has created a negative ripple effect in the economy. At that particular recession the federal government played a relatively smaller role in combatting it. Leaving it up to the business sector to do the combatting did not turned out very effective since the small and large firms' economic activities were almost at the point of nullifying each other. Unfortunately, the lack of coordination and shared goals by these two groups did not help the economy (Samli 2000). Based on the past experiences, it is necessary for the American economy to develop and follow a counter-recession strategy that would entail a number of steps. Exhibit 7.2 presents a seven-point counter-recession plan for the whole American economy.

- Lay-offs should be minimal if any.
- Instead of lay-offs some reduction in salaries should be exercised.
- Budget cuts and spending reductions are not useful.
- Budget increases in areas where the firm can establish stronger market presence must be used.
- The firm must think of its market position at the end of the recession.
- Instead of worrying about maintaining the same profit picture businesses must use more resources to enhance their market position.
- A critical modification of product and service mixes must be exercised.

Exhibit 7.2   Elements of a proactive business posture.

A National Counter-Recession Plan

The first point in exhibit 7.2 is that businesses should not contribute to and deepen the recession by dramatic downsizing of their labor force. On the contrary, keeping people employed and in fact creating more jobs by reducing work week and job-splitting, by definition, would minimize the impact of recession and would counteract it right at the beginning. Some pay cuts across the board including management salaries may be functional.

Budget cuts and spending reductions are not antirecessionary, they simply refuel recessions. In fact, increases in sales efforts and more vigorous promotional efforts are critical antirecessionary activities. These efforts not only minimize the impact of recession on the firm, but also give a strong position to the firm during the postrecession era.

Increased promotional and sales efforts, by definition, provide a head start for the company during the postrecession period. The proactive company would be in much better competitive position because these efforts have long-lasting effects.

Of course, the firm needs to make sacrifices. The major sacrifice in this case is to reduce profit margins by charging lower prices. Maintaining prerecession sales volumes can be a goal as long as it is understood that expected total revenues are not likely to be the same as that of the prerecession period.

Perhaps, above all, the firm will have to consider which products and services are more necessary for the existing demand in the recessionary period. It may be necessary to make serious adjustments in the firms' product mixes to appeal to the smaller and more selective demands of recessions. Products in recessionary times must become more fuel efficient, maintenance efficient, and above all price efficient. A larger variety of products for the consumers to choose from when money is tight can be a significant antirecessionary orientation by the firm. Another critical step in counteracting recessions is to maintain the core competencies of the firms' labor force by not laying off qualified people. This is called by some as "labor hoarding," which means the best workers in the firm's labor force are maintained despite the economic conditions. This will result in even better product mixes by the firm that are more suitable for consumers in hard times. During a recession part of the conventional unwisdom is laying off expensive workers and hiring cheaper substitutes; this is costly to the firm not only in terms of a loss in core competencies, but also in the time and effort wasted in hiring cheaper substitutes, which is not an efficient way of counteracting recessions (Keynes 1936). It is critical to realize that as the profits dissipate in recessions, the whole company must bear the consequences not only those who are more vulnerable. This means basically that if there are some possible savings everybody in the firm must face the consequences; thus everyone would take a cut in pay, face reduced hours, and the like. If there is such an aggressive counter-recessionary activity the offerings of monetary policy by the financiers can become useful for the firm. Cheap money can help pay for the counter-recessionary efforts.

Proactivity Is a Necessity

If all companies, large and small, were to employ a proactive counter-recession strategy described in exhibit 7.2, then fighting off the recession before it becomes too deep and prolonged will be possible. However, most business executives do not have enough experiences with recessions, since they happen once in a decade or so, and being forced by the financial forces exerted by the 1 percenters or so, do not counteract recessions quickly and effectively.

It is critical for the business community to know more about recessions and what needs to be done immediately. Nucor Company, for instance, exercised a program that was coined "share the pain." It called for pay reductions during recessions up to 20–25 percent for hourly employees. Almost 70 percent of company officers had a pay cut of 35–40 percent. But Nucor never laid off an employee during a recession and appeared to have all of its core competencies intact when the recession was over (Bator 1961; Joyce, Nohria, and Robertson 2005). The company benefitted from this orientation. Once a small company located in Southwest Virginia that produced motors, it survived and prospered during a recession by emphasizing more efficient, less costly, and more versatile products. The company by adjusting its product mix to the conditions of the recession has improved its profitability. It further expanded by creating more jobs.

Because they are extremely costly and because individual business decision-makers do not know much about them, there may be a joint organization at the national level, perhaps as a component one of the governmental organizations, to keep track of a recessionary development or lack thereof.

Our discussion in this chapter has emphasized the demand side of recessions. Although that is the critical side to be concerned about there is also a supply-side discussion. Certain shocks or disturbances in the economy also can cause business recessions. Sudden, very high price of gasoline, for instance, or the negative atmospherics disrupting agricultural output may cause a recession (Bjacek 2006).

All of the examples in this chapter reiterate the need for a counter-recessionary agency pointing out what needs to be done immediately.

Exhibit 7.3 is based on the optimal conditions by the first group of necessary-but-not-sufficient conditions of counter-recession strategies. Many of the conditions and examples presented in this chapter are in perhaps the necessary-but-not-sufficient category. The seven steps presented in the exhibit are sequential in that the whole process

Sequential Steps

1	Early detection of recession
2	Assessing its potential damage for the business and its duration
3	In the immediate run increasing promotional and sales efforts
4	For more prolonged recession modifying product and service mixes
5	For continuing recession, diverting company resources more into promotion and sales efforts
6	"Sharing the pain" type of cost cutting, no exceptions
7	Generating more consumer value for the whole society

Exhibit 7.3   Countercyclical posture by national organization—sequential steps.

may either terminate satisfactorily after the first step, or may go all through the seven specific steps. Going through the seven steps is a display of a full countercyclical economic activity. This may take only a few months or may go on for a number of years. The exhibit figure simply acknowledges the importance of having a strong and coordinated counter-recessionary orientation for the whole society. The exhibit steps need to be understood and implemented. Early detection of a recession is critical so that necessary counter-recessionary activities may take place. Early assessment of how big a recession is could be instrumental for how the counter-recession activity must be presented. If it is likely to be of a short-run duration, strong promotional and sales efforts may be sufficient. However, if it appears to be more a major economic activity then product and service mixes may be modified and more fiscal policy measures may be considered. More and much stronger efforts in promotion of business and sales efforts combined with the earlier activity may become necessary as the recession continues to create economic problem. The firms may get into the "sharing the pain" type of cost cutting. Finally, generating more consumer value for the whole society with all the first six steps of the plan must be considered. This total approach must be implemented without political or economic disruptions (Samli 1993). Perhaps some powerful and aggressive companies such as Nike or Johnson & Johnson may become more market oriented and push forth aggressively the counter-recessionary orientation (Abel and Bernanke 2001).

Summary

Recessions are man made and are man stopped. It is maintained in this chapter that top-down or financially managed recessions use monetary policy and they can be beneficial to the 1 percenters. This enhances the expansion of the finance economy and is against consumer well-being and economic advancement. If however the recession is managed from the bottom up through fiscal policy and tightly guided market economy activities, then the whole society, including the 1 percenters, benefit. The most important point is a coordinated counter-recession strategy that needs to be implemented quickly and decisively.

Chapter 8

Live but Also Learn to Let Live

No individual can become a billionaire without the help, blood, and sweat of many people. Assume a genius who had an idea to innovate a smart phone. There were designers, engineers, manufacturing workers to get the product to the consumer, there were highway construction people. Certainly teachers taught the basics of science, banks extended credit, and police maintained security...I could go on. Even for a genius to develop a product there are many people who are providing the necessary support in many different ways. Thus, it is logical to say that any business successful or otherwise cannot be built by only one person. It takes the proverbial village to keep it going.

Now if we bring this picture to the level of the greedy 1 percenters, it would be not only wrong but also unfair to say that "I built this without any help from others."

As the French say, "liberte, egalite et fraternite," that is, freedom, equality, and fellowship, which are needed for a society to survive, succeed, and prosper. Here, freedom is related to the choice of activities and spent efforts in the economy. Equality, by definition, relates to receiving a fair pay for the efforts that are put forth and partnering or working together to get things done.

The society, any society, has needs that need to be satisfied for successful sustainability and progress. But here the 1 percenters or evil emperors are saying that they are, first and foremost, free and hence they could do whatever they liked. But this is done in a totally unleveled playing field. The 1 percenters claim that the others are not their equals and that they are subservants. They may work together but they do not want them to organize, or develop unions, to reduce their powers. Thus, freedom, equality, and fellowship are not encouraged in the finance economy.

In an earlier book I discussed the problems of the fragile planet; I simply did not realize that the American society is particularly suffering from the presence of these problems and that these problems in time will become even more dangerous.

Problems of a Fragile Industrialized Country

As mentioned earlier, any society has several needs. Satisfying those needs makes the society functional. These needs are not unique to a select few but relate to all members of that society. The fulfillment of these needs cannot be privatized and sold to the highest bidder. Everyone in that society is entitled to the benefits of the fulfillment of the societal needs, but when only the highest bidders benefit, the rest of the society loses. It must be questioned whether we pay money to children to read books or to get good grades? Should we pay people to test risky new drugs? Can we really hire mercenaries to fight our wars; can we sell rights to pollute? Is it proper to auction admission to elite universities? Shall we sell citizenship to wealthy immigrants? These questions and many others can be raised about the practices of the finance economy where there appears to be a price for almost everything (Sandel 2012). All of these issues and many more relate to privatization, which is very prevalent in the finance economy. In other words the financial powerhouses desire all of these and many others be decided upon through privatization. Thus, the first and perhaps the biggest problem for a society to function and progress is having a reasonable solution to the private-versus-public dichotomy (Samli 2009b). Just why do we need to privatize? First, the powerful finance group is not interested in sharing its power with a government. In fact the finance group insists that there should be a small and passive government that will not interfere with the economic conditions. Furthermore, privatization in all situations, as the aforementioned questions show, will make money. So the greed factor is very much in control. If, for instance, education is not free, that is, if we get rid of public education, then knowledge-based information and resultant skills will all be up for sale. This means education will stop being a "right" and will become a "privilege." Certainly this is not acceptable in a democratic society. The society in an economic sense is composed of two groups: wolves and sheep. Uncontrolled, without having a shepherd, the wolves, that is, the 1 percenters, eat the sheep, that is, the 99 percenters. Here the shepherd is the government. It does not have to be big or small; it just has to moderate the interaction between the wolves and the sheep so that no one will be exploited and the future of the society will also be a prime motivator. The government has a major role to play. Despite the objections of the 1 percenters, it is the government that starts the futuristic processes and makes sure that the society does have a future.

The public-versus-private dichotomy is an extremely difficult issue. Although we have much information from the practices of other industrialized countries, we have been labeling them as socialistic and propagandizing freedom, which is called capitalism. Indeed a simplistic orientation of one size fits all should not be utilized. But at the same time allowing the wolves to eat the sheep under the freedom concept as interpreted by the 1 percenters will not provide a glowing future for our society. Currently that is what is happening. The sheep, or as I refer to them as the "forgotten majority" also called the "99 percenters," are losing the battle. Funds and privatization propaganda are making inroads into the societal problems in favor of more revenues for the select few in the short run. The fact that the short run is mentioned a few times here is because it is the orientation of the 1 percenters. It must be realized that there may be more profitable activity for that particular group in the short run. But if they really win, the whole society will lose in the long run.

This is not an argument related to "private is bad" and "public is good," but one to make sure that the society has opportunities to grow and prosper.

It must be strongly reiterated that in some cases privatization cannot even do what is needed. There is no possibility of having a private army to protect the country or totally private education system for the whole society. Similarly, in some situations, private efforts trying to generate profit rather than trying to resolve some of the society's major problems cannot provide satisfactory or even acceptable results. Profiteering from solving the society's problems simply is short-run orientation and will not help the society at all in the long run.

Problems with Privatization

Exhibit 8.1 presents a major list of issues indicating some critical societal areas where privatization is either making major inroads or attempting to make major inroads. There are 11 such areas. Once again this is not an exhausted list nor does it identify a specific priority ordering. But all issues identified in the exhibit are extremely critical for the future of the United States.

The use of technology: It has already been indicated that earlier technology meant an increase in productivity. This increase benefited the society as a whole by generating a one-hour reduction in the work week in every decade. This pattern reversed itself since late 1970s in that the work week became longer and salaries either remained the same or even went down despite the spectacular increase in the productivity of American workers. According to the 1 percenters, increased productivity means a lot of revenue for a select few. This revenue is materialized by using the increase in productivity to replace workers, rather than making everyone more productive. These revenues brought tremendous benefits to 1 percenters as the middle class kept on shrinking. During the past four decades increase in their productivity of American workers has been almost detrimental to them in that many have been laid off so that a few

Factor	Outcome
• The use of technology	• Used by a few to generate economic wealth for a select few
• Deficient infrastructure	• Those who can afford will develop only their needs for a fee
• Distribution of news	• All local newspapers, radio stations, and TV channels are bought and controlled by the financial powers
• Access to education	• Those who can afford will get a good education
• Environmental degradation	• Environmental improvement activities are considered as a cost rather than an investment
• Tax revenues are used for mostly military activities	• Tax revenues are going into militaristic projects
• Merger mania	• Limiting competition rewarding financial powers
• Research and sustainability	• All research activity seems to be used for incremental improvements of the financial giants
• Generation and use of energy	• Status quo generates tremendous profits for the financial giants
• Health care	• Making tremendous profits from people's ailments
• Defense-related production	• Many private companies are making much money by the payments from the defense budget

Exhibit 8.1   The privatization in the fragile economy.

can make money in the short run. The more productive the workers got, the more jobs they lost. This is a deadly scenario, which has been dominating American manufacturing.

Deficient infrastructure: Without a well-managed and fully functioning infrastructure the economy cannot make progress. During the past four decades or so the American infrastructure has been ignored. This is mainly because from the finance group perspective infrastructure development is very expensive even though the American public would benefit from its maintenance and its further development. The finance group prefers the status quo of doing almost nothing. Some companies that are wealthy enough and are facing certain urgency have improved only their part of the infrastructure, which does not reach out to the society and benefit all consumers. However, that group does not quite understand that improved infrastructure would improve the American competitiveness globally (Samli 2010).

Distribution of news: News or information for the populace is extremely critical for people's daily activities as well as for their plans for the longer run. Again, since about the early 1980s local newspapers, local radio stations, and local TV channels are being purchased by the giant finance groups. The end result is that American people are primarily receiving one type of slanted news and no alternative, diverse points of view are readily available. In the fascist society of Hitler's time in Germany there was only one point of view, which was totally biased and led to that society's virtual ruination. We are headed in that direction as well.

Access to education: Education is for the improvement of the society as a whole. It is each individual's "right" to get the necessary education to be the best they can be. Education, up until about four decades ago, was virtually available to everyone at a very low cost. Due to budget cuts for public education and support for private education, in the United States education has become a privilege rather than a right. This type of privatization of the society's education can be profitable for a few groups but is detrimental to the growth of the society. Education should not be a profit-making enterprise. For-profit education does not provide the growth necessary to support economic progress.

Environmental degradation: Organizations such as EPA or the environment protection agency have been in existence for many years. But not only is it facing major budget cuts but it is also being forced to approve the activities of some of the major polluting financial giants. Pollution is something that negatively affects all citizens of the society. The current conditions are encouraging more pollution on the part of major, gigantic coal and petroleum companies.

Allowing these companies to pollute more causes a huge problem. Polluters are making more money and are using their power to limit the laws that would restrict their activities. But the society cannot survive if air, water, and soil are all polluted.

Tax revenues: American national budget has a gigantic military component as if the whole world is out to get us. Not only has the military budget been growing, but it is also, at least partially, absorbing the research and development allocations in the national budget. Although some military-related research activity can be beneficial to the society this is not emphasized. Killing more people at lower cost type of research is simply not beneficial. The military research should not be against the society's advancement. Research and development must benefit everyone in the society rather than some gigantic private companies or some military-related organizations (Samli 2012a).

Merger mania: Perhaps more than anything else, the merger mania has created more harm for the American innovativeness and competitiveness in the world markets. It has reduced competition and made it extremely profitable for financial giants. By the same token, it has also totally disrupted the most powerful all-American industrial fabric. Strong, mean, lean, competing entrepreneurial entities are gobbled up not to benefit the American society but to make some gigantic financial groups even richer. As mergers took place salaries, jobs, and retirement programs all faced a major shrinkage. Thus, merger mania has played a critical role in the shrinkage of the American middle class.

Research and sustainability: In the finance economy almost all research activity leads to incremental improvements to existing products, if any. As mentioned in different places in this book there is no encouragement for bold and far-reaching research to generate major radical innovations. However, this type of existing incrementalism does not deal with sustainability. Sustainability of the US economy is dependent on going beyond the short-run profitability, which the incrementalism may provide. There must be research and plans as to how the future advancement can be achieved. Innovativeness of the society by fostering industrial radicalism must be emphasized at almost any cost.

Generation and use of energy: One of the major area that is threatening the American economy is dependence on other countries for energy. It was President Nixon who emphasized American energy independence. President Carter started renewable energy producing plants. President Reagan stopped all that and renewed the American dependency on fossil fuels. President Bush Jr.'s preferences reinforced this dependency.

Studies have shown that the United States has about 4 percent of the petroleum reserves of the world but utilizes about 25 percent of the world's total supply. The oligopolistic petroleum industry in its private nature is making billions of dollars a year and is using much of its financial force to discourage other types of energy development efforts. This industry is receiving billions of dollars of support to dig holes in American beaches. At this point in time these petroleum giants are making tremendous amounts of money by emphasizing the status quo. But the country needs its own renewable energy, which is almost totally blocked by the 1 percenters. The desperately needed replenishable energy based on wind, sun, animal excrement, and trash are almost totally ignored as being expensive. But, with industrial advancements their cost could be reduced. The BP incident, which cost billions of dollars to American consumers during 2008–2011, wasted enough resources, which could have been used to develop any one of these renewable energy industries. Above all we the tax-paying consumers gave billions of additional dollars to the petroleum oligopoly to dig more holes in our wonderful beaches.

Health care: A society cannot function without providing health care to its population. Here however, the private financial giants are determined to control it. This means a few groups making big profits by keeping the health care system private. We in this country are paying at least twice as much for health care as a percent of GDP than any other industrialized country. All other industrialized countries have a public health care system managed by a single payer. In the United States an oligopolistic group of private health care insurance companies are making a lot of money by taking advantage of people's ailments. These oligopolists are not at all providing health care but are collecting about 30 percent of all the health care spending.

Defense-related production: Not only does the defense have the biggest budget portion in the national budget, but this budget is providing major sums to private companies that are producing for the defense of the country but charging exorbitant sums and producing somewhat unneeded products and services at prices that are hurting the rest of the economy. The forces keeping these activities private are winning. The national defense of the country from that perspective is in the hands of a few private firms who think of their profits much more than the country's defense.

Time to Learn How to Let Live

A country's future cannot be tied to enhancing short-run profitability by privatization. Clearly the future of a country is related to balanced public and private undertakings. While making all public may be communism it will be total chaos to make all activities private.

A country, including the 1 percenters, will be managed very well by the understanding that we all need each other. Billionaires cannot make their money without the help of workers, infrastructures, health care systems, reasonably low-cost renewable domestic energy, and a powerful education system that will produce a well-educated and a productive workforce. The important point here is that clearly you did not make billions of dollars on your own without any help from others. Henry Ford gave high hourly wages to his thousands of workers with the understanding that they may buy Ford cars. The industrial giants must realize that if the common consumers have more money, they will buy more products that will make them richer. If the economy as a whole expands and becomes more promising for all, then it will be beneficial for the millionaires and billionaires as well. In other words the 1 percenters must understand that they cannot survive without the 99 percenters. Hence, learning to coexist is the basic premise of any successful society. I go one step beyond the "live and let live"; I say prosper and let others prosper as well. So, it is not only coexistence but coprogress that has to be the motto.

It must be reiterated that many of the items listed and discussed in exhibit 8.1 are public issues and are handled accordingly in most of the industrialized countries. This must be a lesson to both of the American political parties. The American economy functioned much better during the market economy era than the finance economy era. Perhaps the most important impact of privatization efforts is the fact that these efforts are causing shrinkage in the middle class. The American middle class is becoming almost nonexistent. It must be reiterated that it is the middle class that provides stability to a society. Without it the society becomes unstable and directionless. Privatization and trying to solve societal problems through micro managing is not at all useful or beneficial to the society as a whole.

Summary

Any country has public issues that cannot be managed by privatization. All aspects of the society are, or must be, interactive and working together. It is not a matter of privatization to make much money in the short run, but taking care of the social issues of the society for the future growth and prosperity that needs to be paid attention to. The political parties of the country are so far apart that almost nothing is happening in the American society to take care of the problems that should not be taken care of by privatization as advocated by the financial giants. This chapter presented 11 areas that should not be privatized. Above all, the chapter emphasizes the fact that the 1 percenters do need the 99 percenters. If the two cannot work together we are all in trouble. But it is essential for the 1 percenters to realize that if the 99 percenters are prosperous and happy they will also benefit equally or even more. As the chapter stated it is not only live and let live, but prosper and let others prosper as well. Without such an orientation we do not have much of a future.

Chapter 9

Alice in the Finance Land

Being in wonderland is not likely to be as surprising or shocking for Alice or for most of us 99 percenters as being in the finance land.

The finance land where all things have a price and that price yields a profit for the financial giants is not likely a place where Alice would be comfortable. But we the 99 percent of the society are not comfortable either. Those who are affluent can buy anything, they get first priority, and they don't even know what to do with all that money, whereas people with limited means or no means at all are struggling to survive. Almost half of the people of the finance land are poor. In that land one hundred million plus rely on food stamps for food. But the 1 percenters may be seeking an Indian surrogate mother to carry a pregnancy. They pay $118.00 to emit a metric ton of carbon into the atmosphere. They pay whatever it takes to send their children to the best schools. They pay their hardworking employees minimum wage, which does not yield enough income to survive (Sandel 2012).

Although there is no queen yelling "off with the heads," the 1 percenters are yelling off with their financial power to control politics. They do not want the poor immigrants, or young people among others, to vote since these votes may go against their wishes. They do not approve of people voting based on their college IDs. But they approve the voting of those who have a gun ID.

Questionable Values

Alice will be shocked to find out that the leaders in the finance economy do not believe that women with limited means can or should receive advice from organizations such as Planned Parenthood. They do not believe that women are entitled to manage their bodies and their health. They believe in uninterrupted natural activity, which really means the law of the jungle, will take care of things. So why plan?

An equally shocking fact for Alice is that the leaders of the finance land have certain values about work. Even though many of them have inherited a head start in terms of wealth, education, lucrative jobs, and financial power, they condemn unemployment as some people simply being lazy. Their reaction to very poor street people who are homeless, penniless, and jobless is just "why don't you take a shower and go get a job?" Alice heard these words uttered many, many times.

Instead of selflessness that would be an outcome of being totally independently rich and powerful, the masters of the finance land are extremely selfish. Since they make millions of dollars yearly their motivation is not improving the global competitiveness of their firm but maintaining their jobs for another year or two. So, while the society is not making progress they get richer and that is what they care for.

But they have some very specific values. They do not believe in abortions and they maintain that they take government out of your business, your education, your finances, but by outlawing abortions they put the government into people's bedrooms. Similarly, they are very intolerant with people who do not agree with them about the existing superpower and exactly who it is. Also, they are very intolerant of the people who do not look like them or who speak with foreign accents. They are suspicious of people who do not think like them. They think natural laws will take care of everything and so we do not need a government.

Mischievous Behavior

Alice would wonder how the leaders of the finance land are so different than the rest of the people in that land. The leaders think they need more gold or stocks for speculation and oil for power, while the rest of the people in the finance land need cheap renewable energy, food, and jobs.

These leaders send messages everywhere and try to present themselves as job creators. But they really do not start new entrepreneurial businesses or create new jobs. They don't even make money. They just take it. They are making almost unimaginable fortunes by skimming money from their customers. They don't even think of the responsibility of serving their customers and giving them some value. They take money and give virtually nothing in return (Ratigan 2012). But by sending a message that they are job creators they expect additional tax breaks from the government. In fact, they get those breaks.

Creating Crises

Another surprising observation of Alice is that the leaders of the finance land basically create crises and benefit from them. Alice noticed at least four types of crises created by these leaders: job crises, housing crises, energy crises, and food crises.

Alice noticed that when the economic times get a little harsher, the leaders start laying off their workers. They do that primarily to maintain their own financial status by cutting cost and creating unemployment. They do not look at alternatives such as expanding business, developing job-splits to create more employment or having pay cuts to keep the economy going without creating severe hardship by having unemployment.

The leaders of the finance economy created a housing bubble, which became a crisis. They sold millions of expensive homes to the people who could not afford to buy them. The end result of such a situation was that millions of these homes were repossessed or people are living in homes that they cannot afford. Payments and paper value of these homes are much higher than their actual current value in the housing market.

Alice was quite surprised when she found out that the leaders of the finance economy own the fossil fuel resources and do not allow renewable energy sources to develop. The fossil fuels make the owners extremely rich while making the society more and more in debt. Alice found it even more surprising that the companies that are creating fuel energy are receiving billions of dollars of tax advantages over and beyond the billions of dollars they are receiving in terms of profit. As the supply is limited and the dependency on fossil fuel is growing, the profitability of the fossil fuel oligopoly is getting to be out of site.

Finally, the first three crises: jobs, housing, and energy are creating a food crises. Poorer consumers are concentrating on the cheapest available foods for survival and the prices of even these are rising. All of these crises made the leaders of the finance land richer. The cheap available foods are produced by the industrial leaders. They thrive on the misery of the poor.

More Social Issues

Alice kept on thinking that the leaders of the finance economy should be sympathetic to people's needs and their problems; however, she found out that these leaders were totally against social security, Medicare, and especially Medicaid. They were against a national retirement program or social security. If there is no national retirement program, they will be able to sell private retirement programs and make huge profits.

Something for Medicare: If there is no national medical care, then people will be forced to buy private medical insurance programs from the oligopolists, and these oligopolist firms will make incredible profits. The same thing for Medicaid. If you do not have means to buy medical care, too bad.

Summary

One morning Alice woke up and looked around. She said to herself, "Oh my gosh! It was certainly a long, bad dream, really a nightmare.

I don't see how there could be a country like that. Those finance land leaders are totally out of touch with people. They are extremely greedy and that country cannot survive the way it is run. Perhaps it is my imagination and there is no such country. I never thought the wonderland is good, but instead of fighting with greedy financial leaders I would rather put up with the EVIL QUEEN."

Chapter 10

Government: A Partner or Foe?

In all of the industrialized countries the government is a fully pledged partner. In some it is even a leader. However, in our society the government is looked upon as an enemy. Although this is primarily the orientation of the 1 percenters, many 99 percenters also consider it being not very friendly.

One percenters consider the functioning of capital at least in three controversial ways. First, capital accumulation is a basic event in the history of mankind. It has had an unstoppable power march through the world to create a single system of production and distribution. Second, it has its own power in that accumulated capital tends to reduce previously established forms of status, title, and privilege. Third, the laws by which capital functions, although part of the existing legal system, are paid more attention to in capital's favor (Hardt and Negri 2000).

These conditions particularly in the United States provide a power base for the 1 percenters and have been carried out to an extreme in the creation of a finance society. Although some of these points are discussed in different parts of this book, it is important to reiterate that, in a much more practical sense, 1 percenters like to have a small government. Small governments become powerless as opposed to big financiers. Thus, the small government cannot establish rules that would limit the practices of financiers. Small governments can establish and implement progressive income taxes, which

1 percenters think are confiscatory and should be flat and very low. This antigovernment sentiment becomes totally recognizable and acted upon powerfully in the finance economy. Thus, financiers look upon government not as a partner or leader but as an enemy to cope with. They try everything to counteract the government's decisions and to block its actions.

Government as a Partner

Again, although many of the points in this section are touched upon in different parts of this book they should be brought together in one effort.

Exhibit 10.1 presents a 10-point list of the key areas that the society needs help for from a powerful and fair government that functions as a partner. One percenters maintain that all of these functions should be privatized and nongovernmental. Of course, that means they could make tremendous amounts of money for taking over these functions.

Development of new technologies: As discussed in different sections of this book government typically is an initiator of new technologies by providing funds and support. Instead of the US economy the Chinese and Singaporean governments are doing this for their

- Development of new technologies
- Economic storms
- Investment in start-ups
- Helping globalization
- Creating powerful national economy
- Regulating financial markets
- Research and development budgeting
- Social safety net in issues
- Supporting for education
- Creating and supporting technology changes

Exhibit 10.1   The most important nonmilitary government functions.
Source: Adapted and revised from Thurow (2000).

countries. In the United States the emphasis by the pressures of 1 percenters is on existing technologies and their militarization. The military budgets are supporting defense-related private enterprises owned by the 1 percenters. Thus, there is no emphasis on the future of the country and its economic progress through radical innovations.

Economic storms: As has been maintained by many economists, spending more if there is a recession and spending less if there is a boom is the major orientation. If particularly spending more and on more appropriate industries are done early enough by following early indicators the recessions that are very costly and disruptive could be eliminated. Again this type of economic and governmental maturity is not displayed in reality since the two American political parties are not partners and hence the society has only half of a partner. The other half is blocked by the opposition party.

Investment starters: Small entrepreneurial enterprises are perhaps the most critical factor in economic growth. In many societies this factor is financed, supported, and maintained by the government. In such cases, the government's critical role in that society's economic well-being cannot be understated.

Help globalization: Globalization for some countries has been the key for economic development. The four Asian tigers, Singapore, Hong Kong, South Korea, and Taiwan, have had their economic development accelerated through their involvement in globalization. The government in these countries has played a very active role in the country's playing a critical role in the global trade expansion.

Creating powerful national economy: Any country that is excelling in its economic development, that is establishing a name as an economic power would have its government playing a critical role. Without their government's participation in their economy Germany or Japan, among many other countries, would not have the progress they have made in their economic arenas.

Regulating financial markets: As financial markets in original market economies emerged, governments played a key role as to financing work, productivity, and economic growth. Regulated and somewhat controlled financial activities provided the necessary financial impetus for economic growth and development.

Research and development budgets: It is the knowledge that generates the basic and critical breakthroughs in technology that would practically change the world. Being curious, wanting to explore, willing to learn, and wishing to develop are all necessary ingredients of knowledge development without which economies cannot develop or advance. The knowledge development is very critically connected to research and development budgets (Thurow 2000). Particularly at the beginning of knowledge development very high cost and risky research and development activities become major governmental areas to support. Without such support, once again, economic progress may not take place.

Social safety net issues: Societies do not organize themselves without guidance from a leader that is likely to be the government. Maintaining public order, building and maintaining the necessary infrastructure, delivering health services are all critical areas that a functional and proactive government is typically involved with in a progressive society.

Support for education: If knowledge is important for the advancement of a society, and it certainly is, support for education is a necessity. All members of the society must have access to education to become more creative, problem-solving, decision-making productive individuals. Without education there cannot be progress; without government support for education there is no likelihood that the necessary knowledge base can be generated and obtained by the populace.

Creating and supporting technology changes: The knowledge base and the skills required to use this knowledge depend upon new and fast-moving technologies. Many of these technologies have to be created and certainly maintained jointly by the government, the education system, and the private sector. Thus, once again, the undeniable need for the services of the government as a partner becomes an unavoidable fact of progressive life (Thurow 2000; Samli 2012).

Changing Status

As has been discussed in different sections of this book, the change from a market economy to a finance economy has changed the status and the role of the government. In the market economy all of the functions of government, discussed earlier, were not only welcomed but also solicited. Here the government played the role of a full-fledged partner and even more, in the sense that in the Kennedy or Clinton administrations, the government had more of a leading role than a that of a partner.

As the finance economy gained more momentum the government moved from being a partner to playing an almost subservient role in the sense that most of the decisions to create economic momentum were blocked by the financiers since they did not want a change in the status quo. Financiers tried to gain the government's power and use it to their advantage. This describes the current situation of the economy.

A Philosophical Stance

No business or organization can make successful decisions without a powerful and capable administration. It is somewhat out of line to think that a country should be managed not by a government but should be micro managed by some financial powers. This is a dangerous orientation for the future of a country, any country.

For discussion purposes I use the following example. Consider having 50 best musicians (or 50 states) in one room and 50 mediocre musicians in another. Both are to play Beethoven's fifth. The best musicians do not have a conductor but the mediocre group has Zubin Mehta (a very well-known conductor) as a conductor. The question now is: which group will produce a better Beethoven's fifth. Quite correctly, invariably, students would say the mediocre group. Here the conductor is the government. Of course the government has to be qualified enough to be an effective conductor. But without a conductor even the best cannot be at their best. Thus government, a qualified and capable government, must not only be present as a partner but must be a conductor to unite and coordinate the efforts of the players (or the states).

Summary

This chapter could have been at the beginning of this book. Regardless where it is placed, it deals with the fact that without good management any organization cannot make progress. Government is the management of the country. During the past four decades or so, its role and status have deteriorated. It is not any government that is big or small but a government that is proactive and progressive that is needed.

Chapter 11

Going Forward to a Market Economy

Just what now? The finance economy, although extremely profitable to some in the short run, is self-destructive and is even gaining momentum temporarily. This situation is not sustainable. It may be maintained that this is a general indicator for the American society. Unfortunately, very little happens in our society until an issue becomes a very critical problem. But, in this case, we simply cannot afford to wait to the point where there may be no other alternatives. Although the general problem of an emerging and growing finance economy has been in the making for about four decades it still is not hopeless. But it is necessary to counteract this very dangerous movement before it totally destroys our society. Just how can this be accomplished? The first and foremost activity is to create a powerful government that is fair and would level the playing field for all Americans and not just for the 1 percenters. Indeed, the financial leaders object to having a big government so that they can do more of what they are doing without interruption from regulations and conditions. It must be understood that the government must be big and powerful to counteract the financiers' outrageous demands such as billionaires needing a major tax cut. Having a powerful federal government, through propaganda, has become an un-American concept with which many in our society are threatened as socialism or fascism will take over. Thus it is not likely to become a reality. The controlling 1 percenters could be made an un-American concept, which is also not likely to happen. What can happen is that both of the political parties can get together and work for the society.

How can we level the playing field without a central authority so that all Americans will have equal opportunities for jobs, for education, for health care, and for retirement? This perhaps is the biggest challenge. But how do we improve a society where big money is spending more on jails because that is a source of big profits, or big money insists the corporations are people and so they are free to spend billions of dollars to influence the outcome of elections. This is not describing a democracy where each vote counts. This is the description of a finance society that is run not by a government but by billions of dollars. If there is possibility for improvement that will happen when money is taken out of politics and used to support small entrepreneurial businesses to create jobs and to level the playing field. Can this be done without a, God forbid, civil war? In many societies history tells us that similar situations led to domestic civil wars. No society is immune to this kind of a situation.

Let's assume that we are lucky enough to take money out of politics, and then we may start what I call the "marketization process." Exhibit 11.1 presents an eight-step model that is needed to be taken extremely seriously. As a society if we truly want to make progress, to survive and prosper these steps are essential.

- Taking money out of politics
- Using budgets as economic tools
- Making GDP more equitably distributed
- Making education accessible for all
- Making corporate entities smaller
- Making competition untouchable
- Making innovational breakthroughs possible
- Emphasizing both capital and labor

Exhibit 11.1   Steps of moving forward.

Using Budgets as Economic Tools

Currently, the financiers are totally intolerable with budgetary deficits, particularly at the federal level. They think that deficits mean we are borrowing too much and surpluses mean revenues earned by their own money and hence must be distributed to the wealthier in the society. But actually budgets are not to be balanced; they are tools to be used according to economic conditions. When, for instance, there is a recession there has to be much borrowing that will create a deficit in the budget. But the extra money through borrowing would be used exclusively for job creation by smaller and ambitious companies so as not to outsource jobs and innovations but generate domestic jobs and innovations. On the other end of the spectrum if there is a surplus the money should go to areas such as infrastructure, most promising industries, most job creating companies and, perhaps above all, education for everyone.

But the budget, regardless of economic conditions, must have a component that Drucker (1980) named "opportunity budgeting." This is one portion of the federal budget that is to be set aside to create opportunities for the most suitable and promising opportunities for the private sector. Here, identification and prioritization of the changing and newly emerging opportunities are particularly emphasized. This is quite beyond the standard operational budget development. While the operational budgeting takes care of the standard and traditional budgeting activities, opportunity budgets would give the highest rate of return for efforts and expenditures. This type of proactive budgeting is a must to cultivate the most promising and most suitable opportunities for the private sector (Samli 1993). The same opportunity budgeting concept should also be used by enterprises themselves since they are the ones to innovate and produce. Meaning that every business should have as a part of its budget an opportunity budget where explorations for future development are financed. Thus budgets are not only proper economic tools to manage recessions or booms but also tools to be used in economic progress nationally and locally.

Making GDP More Equitably Distributed

Since effective demand is based on buying power it is of utmost importance that consumers have money to buy things that would satisfy their needs.

As mentioned in different sections of this book having money in the hands of the lower-income groups ensures that basic products that are needed for survival and continuation of life, such as food, apparel, pharmaceuticals, and the like, will be sold immediately; this means that the economy is functioning well. In the Keynesian terminology (1936) those people who have a greater propensity to consume will do it quickly. This means at least three basic necessities need to be present. First, the income distribution within the country has to be more equitable, those who make more also pay more income tax. This particular provision should not be a political tool to get elected. Inequitable income distribution creates a major economic imbalance. If the society is experiencing a very deep discrepancy between the incomes of the rich and the poor, this will be a situation that needs to be remedied before it becomes a civil war.

The second condition for those who display higher propensity to consume is job security. This means instead of creating unemployment by laying off workers in recessions every effort must be made to maintain employment levels high. By creating job splits, reduced work week, or cut in pay, job security may be maintained even though these options may not be very desirable.

The third condition for higher propensity to consume workers, in general, is that there must be reasonable wages so that the workers will spend enough. In a society it is not how much billionaires make but how much the average worker makes that is important. If large numbers of consumers are receiving wages that are not at all increasing but the cost of living is going up then the society is rather dormant economically speaking. Without workers receiving reasonable wages that would reflect the worth of their toil there will be no economic progress. How much the average worker is making and how much increase or decrease in that earning level is taking place indicates if the economy is in the right direction or not. That means a fair distribution of the GDP is essential for economic progress. This is a point that 1 percenters must learn to appreciate.

Making Education Accessible to All

The more educated people are, the more productive they become. Education is the key in developing and improving human resources of the society. Developing human resources has at least three distinct impacts on consumers' well-being and, commensurately, on the empowerment of consumers in our society. First, better education makes it possible for individuals to make more money and to have a better quality of life. The difference between a high school education and a college degree is approximately one million dollars in one's productive lifetime. Similarly, the difference between a college degree and a master's degree is estimated at another one million dollars throughout the productive life of an individual. Thus, through education, individuals make more money, and the economic base expands. Second, if they are better educated, all individuals in a society make better and more efficient decisions. This leads to the overall betterment of society. Third, almost half of Americans at the writing of this book are estimated to be below the poverty line. Most of them can be rescued by better or more education and training. Improving the economic status of these people will contribute significantly to the enlargement of the total American economy and its potential growth. The rumors are such that there are millions of jobs that are not filled because not enough quality workers are available. This is a deadly scenario for the American economy's global competitiveness. China and India, among others, are way ahead of us at this point in time in terms of emphasizing education for future growth.

What seems to be blocking educational advancement? While the globalization and advancement in technology are demanding better education and complicated skills, the American education system is

- Attempt to privatize
- New and more demands on budgets such as cost of incarceration
- Several attempts to control education by the people who are not quite qualified
- Inability to attract the best talent to teaching
- Changing goals and practices of the system

Exhibit 11.2   Counterprogressive factors in American education.

falling behind. Exhibit 11.2 illustrates five dramatic activities blocking advancement in our education system.

Attempts to privatize education by the financial powers in our society have been going on for about three decades or more. As has been said earlier, making education a privilege is very profitable. But education is the natural right of all citizens and the society depends on it. Above all education cannot be and should not be for sale.

Making education strictly a budgetary item and making it compete with other items in the budget has become a common practice during the past three decades or so. Unfortunately, some states such as California are paying more for incarceration than for education. This is a disastrous situation. Earlier, education did have a higher status in the budgets. States appeared to be almost competing as to which one can provide better education for the youth. Those days are long gone. If they cannot be brought back, the American society has a very questionable future.

Controlling education locally has become almost a political game. Local education boards that make decisions on educational activity are typically loaded with people who are not qualified to make such important decisions about education that would determine the future of our society. Making a political football of education must stop immediately. Additionally, particularly in universities, administrators who are receiving exorbitant salaries but are not quite qualified as educators must be given more educational input. They have to become more education oriented rather than finance oriented.

Almost all of the aforementioned situations are making it totally difficult to attract the best talent to the noble profession of teaching.

Teachers and professors are constantly under pressure by administrators, politicians, and even churches. Education is to improve human resources of the society not to promote any political, financial, or religious point of view.

Finally, while education has been of the highest priority in the past, the orientation toward it has changed. Unqualified people making key decisions on the education system are discussing how to cut the education budget rather than how to improve the nation's education level.

The idea of a learning society stems from learning organizations. Organizations that are progressive and that excel in the economy must once again be emphasizing the concept of learning organizations rather than finance organizations. In order for our society to become a learning society, as it was before, it must perform at least five key functions.

In addition to stopping the counterprogressive forces listed in exhibit 11.2, our education system must accomplish at least five additional tasks. First, it must broaden the knowledge level so that our society will be, once again, ahead of other societies. Second, it must spread knowledge among American companies and the society as a whole. Third, it must create career opportunities through education. Fourth, it must develop better understanding of scientific language so that people will be appreciative of scientific advances. And fifth, it must invest more time and effort to create a more educated and sophisticated society (Samli 2001). This total orientation is extremely important for the society as a whole. The financiers also will be better off as the society makes significant progress in its education system. But they have to recognize this and that is at least partially the responsibility of the education system.

Making Corporate Entities Smaller

By emphasizing a somewhat smaller corporate entity the society not only avoids the situations of too big to fail or too big to succeed but, above all, increases and maintains competition in the economy. The emphasis of the society should not be regulating or deregulating but enhancing competition and legally enforcing that competition.

Exhibit 11.3 puts forth a series of conditions that appear to be not considered in the finance economy. The finance economy believes in not having laws. It claims that all laws are restrictive in terms of corporate functions. However, some corporate functions must be restricted for the benefit of the society as a whole. In other words, corporate entities are not a bunch of angels thinking of the beneficial activities to benefit the society. In the finance economy corporations are more concerned with their immediate revenues than the society's well-being. Exhibit 11.3 describes what needs to be done to enhance competition in the economy, which will provide a well-functioning economy making progress for survival and prosperity in the future.

Principles to Maintain or Enhance Competition	Needs
To stop monopolies or attempts to monopolize	To stop merger mania
To stop practices deliberately trying to create monopoly power	To prevent price discrimination, manufacturers' power over distributors, to enhance fair trade laws
To stop any attempts to hurt competition	To establish and implement certain conditions to block activities that might hurt competition
To stop separate state-specific practices that may be considered fair in one state and unfair in another	To develop and implement across-the-board fairness in grade and economic activity
To prohibit economic power or asset acquisition that may hinder competition	To make sure that companies cannot use excessive power to hurt their competitors
To prevent practices that would mislead consumers and discriminate against them	To establish parameters of fairness that would enable individuals to make better decisions without being misled or exploited

Exhibit 11.3   Conditions leading to laws to enhance competition.
Source: Adapted and revised from Samli (1993).

Perhaps, above all, by maintaining a healthy level of competition not the financiers but American consumers will be empowered. Perhaps the most obvious condition is to stop monopolies and all attempts to monopolize. Some of the most obvious aspects of merger mania need to be stopped. Also when certain firms become too big to succeed and are tempted to monopolize they must be broken into multiple competing firms. Although antitrust laws have been dealing with these issues, during the past three decades or so they have not been strenuously enforced.

Creating a monopoly or attempting to create a monopoly is not as common as some firm's creating excessive economic power that is monopolistic through certain practices. Practices such as price discrimination and manufacturers' excessive power that is used to keep dealers and distributors in control are strong hindrances to competition and are not controlled by laws. Trade discounts must be fair and available under similar situations to everyone. Otherwise, small retailers cannot compete with larger retailers, and small wholesalers cannot compete with large wholesalers.

Although the first two items in exhibit 11.3 deal with these conditions, it is also necessary to have a general parameter regarding competition. Any attempt that will lessen or hurt competition must be stopped. It is critical also to establish uniform criteria that will not change from state to state and that will be administered and implemented locally. Since attempts to hurt or lessen competition may vary from one locality to another, it is critical to provide local flexibility within the prescribed guidelines.

At the same time, individualized state-specific practices that are considered "fair" may vary so much from one state to another that they may create confusion and inconsistency. Thus, across the board, fairness in dealing with competition and the well-being of consumers must be reexamined and certain general criteria must be established so that fairness in the trade within and between states will always be present.

Companies must be using their economic power not to acquire assets or the economic power of others but to develop new methods, new techniques, and new products; in short, they must innovate.

Finally, exhibit 11.3 posits that certain practices that would mislead consumers or discriminate against them in different ways must be prevented. This will call for establishing parameters of fairness that would enable individual consumers to make better decisions without being misled or exploited.

Exhibit 11.3 does not necessarily present an exhaustive list. It certainly does not imply the need for many more laws that may hinder good decisions or style initiatives. However, certain behaviors on the part of the business sector are described through the conditions specified in exhibit 11.3 and are typical behaviors in the finance economy. Unless such behaviors are eliminated the economy cannot empower consumers and enhance their quality of life (Samli 2001). About four decades ago there was an office of consumer affairs at the federal level, which had offices in many states. However, despite the fact that life is much more complicated, these offices do not exist and consumers in the finance economy do not have protection.

Making Competition Untouchable

Although we claim that we are a society of laws, as discussed earlier, the laws that are designed to protect competition are hardly enforced. However, we the society need not be protecting competition but enhancing it so that there will be progress.

If the conditions and laws presented in exhibit 11.3 were to be present and enforced the American economy's competitiveness will be untouchable and society will move on forward. Without such parameters the established American economy will continue being controlled by the 1 percenters and its future would be bleak.

Making Innovational Breakthroughs Possible

Perhaps the most critical aspect of the competition that existed in the market economy is, at least partially, reflected in the society's innovativeness. It is absolutely critical for the economy to move forward to generate major innovational breakthroughs, which will start not only new business but also new industries. That kind of dynamism requires radical innovations that should be supported by opportunity budgeting, discussed earlier. Radical innovations don't happen all by themselves; much effort goes into developing disruptive technologies that bring about radical innovations. Thus, much preparation goes into the development of radical innovations. Here, not worrying about immediate returns to investments but planning for future development is the key. This orientation is absolutely a must for a dynamic society with a very promising future. Such situations necessitate major governmental help that would make the innovational breakthroughs possible.

Emphasizing Both Capital and Labor

It is not clear why it is capitalism and not laborism. Without labor capital cannot do much but without capital labor also is not of much use. The financiers and many government officials do not realize that today's capital is yesterday's labor. If we understood these two and how they interact our society will be better off. The 1 percenters believe only in capital, particularly their own, but if they could comprehend that a well-treated and fully functioning labor force would make their capital more productive and more profitable, then our society will be in a much better state. The future of any society cannot be determined and formed without a proficient labor group. If both capital and labor are coordinated, reinforcing each other and also progressive, the society will be in a good economic shape.

Perhaps before we finish this chapter, we must ask just how sustainable our economy is now and how sustainable it should idealistically be. The critical issue for the 1 percenters is not to think how much money they have now or how much more can they get next year, but if we as a company or as a country can survive in the longer run. They owe it not only to themselves but to the whole society to ask just what our social, environmental, and economic responsibilities for survival are (Haugh and Talwar 2010). If the society does not survive the accumulated wealth would mean nothing. It must be understood that financial sustainability is, therefore, secondary to social and economic sustainability. When our economy moved from being a market economy to becoming a finance economy the social and economic sustainability of both were underminded completely and the social and economic sustainability was replaced by making money in the short run. The concerns, in other words, unjustifiably moved toward financial sustainability in the short run. The upper left quadrant of exhibit 11.4 describes the situation that is currently haunting the American economy, which is a fully functioning finance economy presenting numerous too-big-to-failers, overemphasizing financial well-being in the short run, and not even knowing the impact of their activities in the long run. The lower left quadrant of the exhibit illustrates that if the current conditions continue, in the long run the too-big-to-failers will fail. Money and wealth would accumulate in the hands of a few, which will create no opportunities to start and expand businesses and a very dangerous conflict between the haves and the have-nots will take place.

The upper right quadrant of exhibit 11.4 indicates that in the short run the corporate entities must put more emphasis on corporate social responsibility of creating more jobs, paying good wages,

	Financial sustainability	Economic and social sustainability
Short-run	Too big to fail Overemphasis on financial measures Not paying attention to long-run	Needed emphasis on corporate social responsibility Modifying their concerns and supporting economic well-being
Long-run	Too big to fails Money accumulates in the hands of a few Not enough demand for businesses to run	Having healthy corporate social responsibility The middle class will be thriving The society becomes dynamic and market oriented again

Exhibit 11.4   The sustainability question.

supporting major innovations, and many other behavioral issues. If they modify their concerns and support the society's economic well-being, the lower right quadrant of the exhibit indicates that a healthy corporate social responsibility will take place and a thriving middle class will reappear and the society as a whole will become dynamic and market oriented again. Thus the exhibit indicates where we are and where we should be going.

Summary

This chapter is a blue print of the progress needed for the American economy to get out of its dormant and deteriorating situation. It must be pointed out that the chapter maintains the need for a dynamic economy moving forward to a set of market economy conditions. It is maintained that an eight-step dynamic plan will put our economy in a better shape than it ever has ever been in. Certainly unlike the leaders of the finance economy, it is maintained here that a potentially very dynamic society cannot be run by a group of millionaires and billionaires who do not want a major change. They are oriented toward having quick financial revenues in the short run without even thinking of the country's, and for that matter their own, future. They are status quo oriented. This chapter points out that this mold must be broken for the society and its people so that once again American economic dynamism will take over. Clearly without an objective, informed, and powerful government and an informed and dynamic business sector the wishful dream of moving forward to another phase of a progressive market economy is simply a dream. Sustainability must be emphasized as vigorously as possible.

Postscript

Here we are in a most progressive society with a most regressive government. We have too many people and too few jobs and the jobs are paying less and less. The issue of having too many people was not brought up in this book. But, only the third-world countries and the United States don't have a general population policy. Besides having too many people, lawlessness and greed are running rampant in our society. This society with its greedy and not too well-educated financial bosses has almost no place to go. Certainly, as has been described in the book, there are wolves and sheep but where is the shepherd? Wolves clearly are eating the sheep and nothing is being done about it. Constant talk about "freedom" is everywhere but whose freedom are we talking about? Certainly when big banks gamble away their customer's money they are free but those who are losing their money are not. Not only does everyone in our society not have equal opportunity but the tyranny of the 1 percenters is obvious and is getting worse. They have the freedom, but the 99 percenters, or the rest of the society, do not.

One percenters always talk about small government. There really are not too many good explanations about the shepherd mentioned earlier being a midget. This would not work. Big government! God forbid; it is socialism but so is having a national army, a national education, a national retirement program, and the like We don't need a big or a small government; we need a good government that represents all the people, protects all the people, and truly *governs*. Just when and, more importantly, how are we going to wake up? This is a tremendous society with tremendous potential but the 1 percenters are exploiting these potentials and literally enslaving the remaining 99 percent of the society.

Just nobody explains why income tax should be flat. In the 1950s the highest income tax rate was 92 percent. Millionaires paid that much of their income and the country did well. Somehow we must get our societal affairs in order. It appears that we are headed for some serious turbulence by creating a tremendous gap between the rich and the poor in our society.

We simply cannot afford to have a group of greedy people determining the direction in which our country is headed and how the people should work exclusively for their profit. After all, they may become generous enough to offer us a job, which would not even pay enough to help us take care of our children or ourselves.

How could a CEO makes hundreds of millions of dollars when the minimum wage is not even 10 dollars or the average earnings of his/her workers is some three hundred times smaller?

As if the financial inequality is not enough, these financial powerhouses decide what and how schools and universities must be conducted and what kind of education our youth should have. But they themselves are too uneducated and uninformed to pass a judgment in this all-important area. If we do not have a well-prepared, powerful youth, we as a society do not have a future. Education simply is not for sale. It is not a privilege. Everyone in the society is entitled to as much education as the individual can absorb.

The one percenters who for some reason or other are extremely wealthy look down on the poor people. They think, in fact they believe, that it is through their own fault that they are poor. But then one percenters have been born with a golden spoon in their mouth, they have never been poor. So they cannot empathize at all with the problems of the poor. They don't think the society owes anything to the poor; if they are sick and hungry, well, let them die. But if they are alive and well they must work for them at slave wages.

Further they question why everyone who has worked diligently for many years should have a retirement program. After all if there is a retirement program it would limit the financiers' almost unlimited income growth. The greedy financiers say that I got mine and if they cannot get theirs, let them be damned. Having a finance economy thus entrusts the power of ruling and managing the society to money.

This is not quite acceptable. Ours, however misguided it may be, is a wonderful society with tremendous potential that is all not lost yet. What our society needs is a government that is not for sale and will govern some important laws to be constructed and enforced so that people cannot take advantage of each other. It further needs a progressive income tax; the 1 percenters must pay taxes proportionate to what they receive from the total GDP. Our society, once again, must reward capability and performance rather than riches. Our population must be functioning on a well-balanced, fair, and totally leveled playing field. The future of our country and our people is much more important than the short-run financial gains of a group of privileged people who are spoiled and have no compassion.

Friends, what is truly needed? You be the judge. We must save this society.

A Post-Postscript

In my other books I have not had a second postscript; however, I believe it is very important in this context. After I finished writing the book and before I sent it to the publisher, a statement appeared in the *Bloomberg Business Week* (2012b). It was as follows: "Companies in the Standard and Poor's 500 stock indexes with the exception of banks and utilities are *rolling in cash*, over 1 trillion during the first quarter of 2012." This is almost a record. What would these companies do? Instead of expanding, starting major innovations, and above all creating more jobs, they simply are not planning on investing more and adding new employees. But, as I question throughout the book, why? Because they really don't have to. If they do not spend more, there will be more left for the 1 percenters. In fact the article in the journal goes on to say that a large number of CEOs indeed planned to cut jobs and spending; of course, by doing so they would maintain their rate of earnings and, of course, who cares for the country or the workers. This is what I have been trying to point out: THE GREED FACTOR. Well! The defense rests.

References

Abel, Andrew B., and Ben S. Bernanke (2001), *Macroeconomics*, Boston: Addison Wesley.

AFL-CIO Executive Pay Watch Calculations (2012).

Alderson, Wroe (1965), *Dynamic Marketing Behavior*, Homewood, IL: Richard D. Irwin.

——— (1957), *Marketing Behavior and Executive Action*, Homewood, IL: Richard D. Irwin.

Bagdikian, B. H. (1964), *In the Midst of Plenty*, New York: Signet Books.

Barton, Dominic (2011), "Capitalism for the Long Term," *Harvard Business Review*, March, 85–91.

Bator, Francis M. (1961), *The Question of Government Spending*, New York: Collier Books.

Bennett, Jane (1998), "Nations Bank to Close II Credit Centers," *Jacksonville Business Journal*, February 13, 49.

Bjacek, Paul (2006), "Lost Manufacturing Resulting in Slower U.S. Pet Chem Growth," *One and Gus Journal*, November 20, 58–63.

Boesky, I. (1985), *Merger mania: Arbitrage*, New York: Holt Rinehart & Winston.

Bloomberg Business Week (2012a), "Barriers to Recovery," September 23, 14.

——— (2012b), "Cost Controls Are One of the Key Reasons Job Growth Remain Relatively Weak," October 8–14, 13.

——— (2012c), "Google-Rola," May 28, 59–61.

Bok, Derek (2006), *Our Underachieving Colleges*, Princeton: Princeton University Press.

Business Week (2004), "Where Are the Jobs?" March 22, 36–47.

Caplowitz, D. (1963), *The Poor Pay More*, London: The Free Press of Glencoe.

Christensen, Clayton M. (2003), *The Innovator's Dilemma*, New York: Harper Business Books.

Chua, Amy (2003), *World on Fire*, New York: Doubleday.

Congressional Budget Office (2012), "Trends in the Distribution of Household Income."

——— (2011), "Trends in the Distribution of Household Income between 1979 and 2007," Washington DC, October, X.

De Brittani, U. (2000), "Innovational Versus Incremental New Business Services Different Keys for Achieving Success," *Product Innovation Management*, December 18, 169–189.

Diebold, Francis X., and Glen D. Rudebusch (2001), "Five Questions about Business Cycles," *FRBSF Economic Review*, 1–15.

Dillard, Dudley (1948), *The Economics of John Maynard Keynes*, Englewood Cliff, NJ: Prentice Hall.

Dodd, Frank (2012), "Too Big to Succeed," *News Bank Access World News*, June, 4.

Drucker, Peter F. (1995), *Managing in Time of Great Change*, New York: Truman Talley.

——— (1980), *Managing in Turbulent Times*, New York: Harper and Row.

Dugger, William M. (1989), "Instituted Process and Enabling Myth: The Two Faces of the Market," *Journal of Economic Issues*, June, 607–615.

Durkheim, Emile (1951), *Suicide*, New York: Free Press.

Engardio, P., Roberts, D., Smith, G., Bard, A., Coy, P., Stokes, J., and Rowley, I. (2008), "Can the U.S. Bring Jobs Back from China?", *Businessweek* (4090): 038–043.

Etzkowitz, Henry, Jose de Mello, Manoel Carvalho, and Mariza Almeida (2005), "Towards Meta Innovation in Brazil: The Evolution of the Incubator and the Emergence of a Triple Helix," *Research Policy*, 34, 411–424.

Friedman, Thomas (2010), "Start-Ups Not Bailouts," *New York Times*, April 4, 9.

——— (2005), *The World Is Flat*, Farrar, Straus and Giroux.

Galbraith, John Kenneth (1956), *American Capitalism*, Boston: Houghton Mifflin Co.

Gaski, John F. (1985), "Dangerous Territory: The Social Marketing Concept Revisited," *Business Horizons*, July/August, 42–47.

Glynn, Mary Ann (1996), "Innovation Genius: A Framework for Relating Individual and Organizational Intelligences to Innovation," *The Academy of Management Review*, October, 1081–1111.

Hansen, Laura L., and SiaMak Movahedi (2010), *Sociological Forum*, June, 367–374.

Hardt, Michael, and Antonio Negri (2000), *Empire*, Cambridge, MA: Harvard University Press.

Haugh, Helen M., and Alka Talwar (2010), "How Do Corporations Embed Sustainability across the Organization?" *Academy of Management: Learning and Education*, September, 384–396.

Hicks, Douglas A. (2004), "Taming the Best: The Virtues of Corporate Life." Review of *William Greider, the Soul of Capitalism* (Simon & Schuster, 2004) and Jonathan B. Wight, Saving Adam Smith (Financial Times/Prentice Hall, 2002). *The Christian Century* 121/6 (March 23, 2004): 24–27.

———. (2004), Reframing the Economics of Pastoral Leadership.

Hill, Ronald Paul, and Deby Lee Cassill (2004), "The Naturological View of the Corporation and Its Social Responsibility: An Extension of the Frederick Model of Corporation Community Relationships," *Business and Society Review*, 3, 281–296.

M. Joseph Sirgy, A. C. Samli, and H. Lee Meadow (1982), "The Interface between Quality of Life and Marketing: A Theoretical Framework," *Journal of Marketing & Public Policy* 1:69–84.

Joyce, William, Nitin Nohria, and Bruce Robertson (2005), *What Really Works*, New York: Harper Business.

Kao, John (2007), *Innovation Nation*, New York: Free Press.

Kennedy, John F. (1963), "Consumer Advisory Council: First Report," Washington DC, United States Government Printing Office, October.

Keynes, John Maynard (1936), *The General Theory of Employment Interest and Money*, New York: Harcourt, Brace and Company.

Kotler, Philip, Somkid Jatusripitak, and Sowit Maesiencel (1997), *The Marketing of Nations*, New York: The Free Press.

Krugman, Paul (1999), Accidental Theorist: and Other Dispatches From the Dismal Science, Princeton University Press.

Lundwall, Glengt-Ake (2007), "National Innovation Systems—Analytical Concept and Development Tool," *Industry and Innovation*, 14, 95–119.

Mandel, M. J. (2009), "Innovation Interrupted," *Business Week*, June 15, 34–40.

——— (2008), "Innovation Economics Shows How Smart Ideas Turn Into Jobs and Growth," *Business Week*, September 22, 52–70.

Manu, Alexander (2007), *The Innovation Challenge*, New York: Pearson Education.

Marx, Karl (1967), *Capital*, Vol. 1, New York: International Publishers.

Morgan, R. M., and S. D. Hunt (1994), "The Commitment-Trust Theory of Relationship Marketing," *Journal of Marketing*, July, 20–38.

Nussbaum, Bruce (2005), "Get Creative," *Business Week*, August 1, 61–68.

Orphanides, Athanasius (2004), "Monetary Policy in Deflation: The Liquidity Trap in History and Practices," *The North American Journal of Economics and Finance*, January, 1–24.

Osborn, A. (1953), *Applied Imagination*, New York: Charles Scriber.

O'Sullivan, A., and Sheffrin, S. (2001), *Economics: Principles in Action*, Prentice Hall.

Perman, Stacy (1998), "Goodbye, Freebies-Hello Fess," *Time Magazine*, January 12, 40.

Pieters, Graeme (2005–2012), Privacy and Cookie Policy, http://moneyterms. co.uk/pareto-optimal.

Plsek, Paul E. (1997), *Creativity Innovation and Quality*, Milwaukee, WI: ASQ Quality Press.

Porter, Michael E. (2008), "Why America Needs an Economic Strategy," *Business Week*, November 10, 39–42.

———(1990), *The Competitive Edge of Nations*, New York: The Free Press.

Prajojo, D. T., and P. K. Ahmed (2006), "Relationship between Innovation Stimulus, Innovation Capacity and Innovation Performance," *R&D Management*, 36, 5, 499–515.

Rand, Ayn (1957), *Atlas Shrugged*, New York: Signet.

Ratigan, Dylan (2012), *Greedy Bastards*, New York: Simon & Schuster.

Reich, Robert B. (2010), *After Shock*, New York: Alfred A. Knopf.

——— (2007), *Super Capitalism, Super Capitalism*, New York: Alfred A. Knopf.

Ryan, William (1981), *Equality*, New York: Vintage Books.

Saez, Emanuel (2012), "Striking Richer: The Evolution of Top Income in the United States," Berkeley, CA: Department of Economics.

Samli, A. C., and J. A. Weber (2000), "A Theory of Successful Breakthrough Management: Learning from Success," *Journal of Product and Brand Management*, January, 35–45.

Samli, A. Coskun (2013), "The Greed Factor: The Insidious Economy That Is Being Ignored," in George Leismuller and Elias J. Schimpf (editors), *Economics of Competition*, New York: Nova Publishers.

———(2012a), "Developing an Innovation Culture," *The Marketing Review*, Summer.

———(2012b), "Generating a Culture of Innovation: The Necessary Ingredient for Economic Progress," *The Marketing Review*, 52, 2, 125–140.

——— (2011), *From Imagination to Innovation*, New York: Springer.

——— (2010), *Infrastructuring*, New York: Springer.

——— (2009a), *Globalization from the Bottom Up*, New York: Springer.

——— (2009b), *International Entrepreneurship*, New York: Springer.

——— (2001), *Empowering the American Consumer*, Westport, CT: Quorum Books.

——— (1998), Marketing Strategies for Success in Retailing, Westport, CT: Quorum Books.

——— (1993), *Counterturbulence Marketing*, Westport, CT: Quorum Books.

——— (1992), *Social Responsibility in Marketing*, Westport, CN: Quorum Books.

——— (1969), "Differential Price Structures For the Rich and the Poor," University of Washington Business Review, Summer, 36–43.

Sandel, Michael (2012), *What Money Can't Buy*, New York: Allen Lane.

Schumpeter, Joseph (1934), *The Theory of Economic Development*, Cambridge: Harvard University Press.

Smith, Adam (2012), *Wealth of Nation*, New York: Simon and Brown.

Stern, Gary H., and Ron J. Feldman (2004), *Too Big to Fail: The Hazards of Bank Bailouts*, Washington DC: Brookings Institution Press.

Stiglitz, Joseph E. (2002), *Globalization and Its Discontents*, New York: W. W. Norton.

Sull, Donald N. (2005), *Why Good Companies Go Bad*, Boston, MA: Harvard Business School Press.

Taleb, Nassim N., and Charles S. Tapiero (2010), "Risk Externalities and Too Big to Fail," *Physical A. Science Direct*, March.

Tan, W. L. (2003), "Entrepreneurship Challenges Ahead for Singapore," in *Entrepreneurship in Asia, Playbook for Prosperity*, Missould, Montana: University of Montana.

Thurow, Lester C. (2000), *Building Wealth*, New York: Harper Collins Publishers.

US Bureau of Economic Analysis (2009), "National Income and Product Accounts": http//www.bea.gov/national/hipaweb/index.asp.

US Bureau of Labor Statistics (2009a), "CPI Detailed Report: Data for August 2009.

———(2009b), "2008 Expenditure Shares Tables."

US Bureau of Labor Statistics' Current Employment Statistics Survey—Table B-2, Average hours and earnings of production and non-supervisory employees on private nonfarm payrolls (2012).

US Census Bureau (2012), Selected Measures of Household Income Dispersion, Table IE-1.

Wachtel, Paul (2003), "Full Pockets Empty Lives: A Psychoanalytic Exploration of the Contemporary Culture of Greed," *The American Journal of Psychoanalysis*, June, 203–233.

Zhang, Y., and I. Yang (2006), "New Venture Creation Evidence From an Investigation into Chine Entrepreneurship," *Journal of Small Business and Enterprise Development*, 13, 160–173.

About the Author

Dr. A. Coskun (Josh) Samli is research professor of Marketing and International Business at the University of North Florida. Dr. Samli received his bachelor's degree from Istanbul Academy of Commercial Sciences (currently Marmara University), his MBA from the University of Detroit, and his PhD from Michigan State University. As a Ford Foundation Fellow, he has done postdoctoral work at UCLA, the University of Chicago, and as an International Business Program Fellow at New York University.

In 1974–1975, he was a Sears-AACSB Federal Faculty Fellow in the Office of Policy and Plans, US Maritime Administration. In 1983, Dr. Samli was invited to New Zealand as the Erskine Distinguished Visiting Scholar to lecture and undertake research at Canterbury University. In 1985, Dr. Samli was a Fulbright Distinguished Lecturer in Turkey. He was selected as the Beta Gamma Sigma, L. J. Buchan Distinguished Professor for the academic year 1986–1987 to work at North Carolina Agricultural and Technical University. He was given a research fellowship by the Center of Science Development, South Africa, February 1995. He was awarded a fellowship by the Finnish Academy of Sciences to teach a doctoral seminar in June 1999. Dr. Samli spent some time serving as a member of Fulbright Commission.

Dr. Samli is the author or coauthor of almost 300 scholarly articles, 25 books, and 30 monographs. He has been invited, as a distinguished scholar, to deliver papers in many parts of the world by many universities. He has lectured extensively in Europe, Eastern Europe, the Middle East, the Far East, Oceania, and many other parts of the world. He was very active in the Fulbright Commission.

Dr. Samli is on the review board of seven major journals. He is the cofounder and the first president and a research fellow of the International Society for Quality of Life Studies (ISQOLS).

Dr. Samli is a Distinguished Fellow in the Academy of Marketing Science and a past chairman of its board of governors. He has done some of the earlier studies on the poor, elderly, and price discrimination. His most recent books are: *From Imagination to Innovation* (Springer 2012); *Infrastructuring* (Springer 2011); *Globalization from the Bottom Up* (Springer 2008); and *International Entrepreneurship* (Springer 2009). Two earlier books: *Social Responsibility in Marketing* (1993) and *Empowering the American Consumer* (2001) were considered among the most important academic books in the United States by *Choice Magazine*, which is managed by librarians.

Dr. Samli has worked with hundreds of small- and medium-sized businesses as a consultant over a 50-year period and he has conducted many seminars for hundreds of business managers and graduate students in Turkey.

Dr. Samli has had more than 25,000 students from all over the world. Many of them are professors, successful businessmen, and statesmen. He reviews dissertations as an outside international expert. Dr. Samli was recipient of Harold Berkman Service to the Discipline Award given by the Academy of Marketing Science in 2008. During the summers of 2008 and 2009 he was the recipient of the Evren Professorship at Florida Atlantic University.

In 2010 he was awarded the first James M. Parrish faculty award at the University of North Florida. Currently, he is in his fifty-third year of professorial activities.

Index

Printed in the United States of America